UNIX GUIDE

FOR DOS USERS

ALLEN TAYLOR

ADVANCED COMPUTER BOOKS

MIS: PRESS

© 1990 by Management Information Source, Inc.

P. O. Box 5277
Portland, Oregon 97208-5277

First Printing
ISBN 1-55828-024-3

Printed in the United States of America

To Lillian Cade, rhetoric and composition instructor at the University of Illinois, who labored at the almost impossible task of teaching engineering students to write clearly.

Contents

Preface

Already the operating system of choice for scientific and engineering users, Unix is clearly on its way to becoming the predominant multiuser operating system for microcomputers, minicomputers, and mainframes. With capabilities that are substantially greater than those of MS-DOS, Unix is rapidly penetrating the high-end business-application niches of the microcomputer market. As more popular DOS applications become available under Unix, its use will spread to the entire business community.

This book provides a quick introduction to the Unix operating environment. Aimed at computer *users* familiar with DOS, rather than programmers, it does not assume knowledge of any programming language. The main purpose of this book is to show new or prospective users of Unix how to exploit its capabilities.

HOW THE BOOK IS ORGANIZED

There are 18 chapters in this book, organized as follows:

Chapter 1 introduces Unix and describes its evolution.

Chapter 2 explains the organizational structure of Unix in layman's terms, giving the reader an appreciation of the differences between Unix and MS-DOS.

Chapter 3 gives you insight into how to set up a Unix system to take advantage of specific hardware features and to provide the capabilities needed for your applications.

Chapter 4 explains how Unix uses disk storage devices.

Chapter 5 covers procedures for backing up and restoring information on the Unix system's disk devices.

Chapter 6 describes logging in and using some of the basic functions in Unix.

Chapter 7 discusses the structure of the Unix file system and explains how to operate upon files.

Chapter 8 introduces the Unix text-processing system.

Chapter 9 describes features related to the multiuser nature of Unix.

Chapter 10 introduces the concept of a process and describes how to control the actions and interactions of processes.

Chapter 11 covers communication with other users on a multiuser Unix system, as well as with remote users on other Unix systems.

Chapter 12 introduces the command shells that provide the user interface to Unix and explains the construction of simple shell scripts.

Chapter 13 describes the tasks that must be performed by the system administrator, the person responsible for the smooth functioning of a Unix installation.

Chapter 14 tells how to set up a system so that MS-DOS applications can be run as tasks under Unix.

Chapter 15 describes how Unix handles the printing of reports and other documents by applications running under Unix.

Chapter 16 enumerates the advanced features of the Unix text-processing system. Text processing is one of the major applications for which Unix was originally developed.

Chapter 17 discusses those Unix features that facilitate the development of application programs. Application programmers were the primary target users of the original version of Unix.

Chapter 18 discusses the X Window system, a graphical user interface that has achieved widespread acceptance on Unix systems.

HOW READERS WILL BENEFIT

Readers who have experience with the MS-DOS operating system will be able to start using Unix quickly because of parallels between the two operating systems, which are pointed out in this book. Unix is a much more complex and feature-rich operating system than DOS, but the two systems have many points in common. Current DOS users will be able to find their way around Unix confidently, once they learn the Unix equivalents of basic DOS operations.

After discussing the basics, the book describes the large number of Unix features that have no DOS equivalents. Because Unix was conceived as a software-development environment, it offers many tools to the third-party programmer. These tools are particularly valuable in the writing of application programs. In comparison, DOS programming tools are quite rudimentary. The book gives the Unix-system user an appreciation of the major facilities that are available to application programmers. Knowledge of those facilities will provide insights into how best to take advantage of Unix applications.

Acknowledgments

I would particularly like to thank The Santa Cruz Operation, Inc. in Santa Cruz, California, and Interactive Systems Corporation in Santa Monica, California, for their help. Without their assistance, it would not have been possible to write this book. I would also like to thank Pailou Chu of Advance Data Systems, in Irvine, California, for supplying me with an affordable 386 platform that runs Unix. Finally, I would like to thank Mike Diaz of Integrated Circuit Technology, Inc. in El Toro, California, for inspiring me to write this book.

Chapter 1

An Overview of Unix

After a long development period at universities, government laboratories, and businesses, the Unix operating system is rapidly rising to prominence. In today's computing environment, which places an ever increasing emphasis on interconnection, Unix is a natural choice—especially for organizations that are trying to make different kinds of computers "talk" to one another. Its ability to run on virtually every kind of computer promises to be the key ingredient that bridges the gap separating microcomputers from minicomputers and mainframes. This chapter traces the evolution of Unix to its current position as the most widely used multiuser, multitasking operating system in the world.

THE EMERGENCE OF UNIX
AS A MAJOR OPERATING SYSTEM

The Unix operating system was originally developed by computer scientists at AT&T in the early 1970s. They intended it for internal use within the Bell system, not as a commercial product. AT&T did, however, give Unix to interested universities. Since the company did not support the copies it gave away, variants developed as universities extended the system according to their own needs.

As computer scientists who had been trained in Unix at these recipient universities entered industry, the Unix operating system became widely known. However, it was the variety of versions, each with its own set of passionate devotees, that hindered the widespread adoption of Unix in industry. Also compounding the acceptance problem was Unix's inability to run on IBM mainframes and personal computers.

Current standardization efforts are finally moving Unix toward the ideal of a single version that incorporates all the best features of the existing variants. Unix is now running well on a wide variety of platforms, including mainframes and the most popular personal computers. In the absence of any serious competition in the multiuser personal-computer market, Unix is experiencing rapid growth in the number of installations; it will soon have a significant market share. Its success has also extended into the minicomputer arena, displacing proprietary operating systems from such companies as DEC and Data General. Unix is already the dominant operating system on engineering workstations, one of the fastest-growing segments of the computer market.

DEFINING AN OPERATING SYSTEM

A computer's operating system (OS) is a layer of software that lies between the computer hardware and the application programs. It can be rudimentary, elaborate, or anywhere in between. The original operating system that was provided for the IBM Personal Computer, PC-DOS 1.0, was definitely on the rudimentary side. The same is true of MS-DOS, the generic version of PC-DOS.

The Development of DOS

PC-DOS 1.0 was built in 1981 by Microsoft Corporation for the 8088 microprocessor around a core developed by Tim Patterson. (DOS stands for Disk Operating System.) In many ways, PC-DOS was similar to the CP/M operating system of Digital Research, Inc. Before the introduction of the IBM PC, CP/M was the most popular operating system on 8080- and Z80-based microcomputers. PC-DOS 1.0 assumed that data was stored either on 5.25-inch floppy disks or on tape cassettes; it provided no support for hard disks.

DOS has come a long way since the introduction of that first version. It is now installed on more than 20 million personal computers around the world. Not only does the current version of DOS support hard disks, it also has become a very sophisticated and powerful operating system. Many thousands of application programs have been written to run under DOS, a fact that provides strong incentives for users to stick with a DOS-compatible system, even as they upgrade their hardware to 80286, 80386, and 80486 machines. The advanced features of these more powerful processors go largely unused, however, since DOS software can be run only in the 8086 emulation mode.

DOS has two other serious disadvantages. First, it is a *single-tasking* operating system; you can work on only one application at a time. Second, DOS is a *single-user* operating system; only one person may use the system at a time.

The evolutionary descendant of DOS is OS/2. Although OS/2 is a multitasking system, it does not support multiuser operation. Furthermore, application software vendors have been slow to support OS/2.

Unix has the opportunity to preempt OS/2 and become the operating system of choice for multitasking applications, as well as for multiuser applications. The large existing library of DOS-based software applications need not be abandoned, since DOS applications can be readily made to run under Unix.

The Development of Unix

Unix was developed long before DOS but did not enter the commercial market during the first decade of its existence. In 1970 (when Unix was developed), AT&T held a legal telephone monopoly throughout most of the United States. To compensate for this, it was prohibited from competing in the computer business. As a result, Unix was not packaged as a product. AT&T used it internally and licensed it to universities that had a computer-science curriculum.

During its development, Unix was not intended to be an adjunct in the selling of computer hardware. Its developers, therefore, were free to design it to meet their own needs. Their primary goal was to produce an environment that facilitated software development. A secondary objective was to create a flexible and powerful text-processing tool. As a result, Unix differed significantly from the proprietary operating systems that preceded it.

Designed *by* computer experts *for* computer experts, Unix was difficult to learn. Since it was not a commercially released product, it was poorly documented. To complicate matters, there was no single standard version. When AT&T licensed Unix to the universities, the schools received complete source code for the system, but no support. These schools, to meet their needs, then started adding their own extensions to the program. Predictably, a multitude of versions proliferated, each with a variety of incompatible features.

Now there is strong support throughout the Unix community for adopting a standard version containing the best features from the most popular variants developed over the years. The success of DOS on personal computers has provided a powerful object lesson in the value of a widely accepted standard operating system. Proponents of a standard Unix foresee similar success with Unix running on a broad spectrum of platforms once a universally accepted standard emerges.

COMPARING UNIX TO DOS

The original version of DOS (1.0) had very little in common with Unix. Designed to run on the 8088, a 16-bit microprocessor, Version 1.0 was very similar to CP/M, which ran on the 8-bit 8080 processor. However, as microcomputer hardware became ever more powerful during the 1980s, DOS was progressively upgraded. Many of those upgrades added Unix-like features to DOS.

Unix Features That Have DOS Counterparts

Perhaps the most important Unix feature that was added to DOS is the *hierarchical file structure*, which was incorporated into Version 2.0. The organization of tree-structured directories is identical in the two systems, and you can navigate between directories using similar (though not identical) commands. Since it is possible to run DOS as a session under Unix on 286, 386 and 486 machines, the consistency of file structure allows you to operate easily on files from both operating systems. In a few instances, minor file-format conversions may be necessary, but utilities to perform such conversions are readily available.

Another feature that is common to Unix and DOS is *pipelining*. Pipelining allows you to issue a series of commands in which the output of each command is the input of the next command.

Of course, both operating systems have commands for basic file-management operations. Although the syntax and function of these commands may differ, Unix can generally perform any operation that DOS can.

Unix Features That Have No DOS Counterparts

Unix Is Multitasking

Unix is a *multitasking* operating system. It contains the commands that allow a user to launch multiple tasks, run them simultaneously, and switch freely between them. DOS has no provision for multitasking, although its successor, OS/2, does. Both OS/2 and Unix let you run multiple processes; each process may contain a separate application program. Since DOS is a single-tasking operating system, it can never execute more than one program at a time.

In a computer with a single central processing unit (CPU), only one program can be active at a given instant. However, the computer can execute thousands, or even millions, of instructions per second. With this speed, it can switch rapidly between several tasks, giving a fraction of a second of execution time to each before passing control to the next task. Such *time sharing* can generally execute a group of programs faster than if they were run sequentially under a single-tasking operating system. This improved efficiency is due to the fact that different tasks (also called *processes*) typically are using different system resources at a given time. If one process is retrieving data from a peripheral device and another is performing a computation, they can both proceed without interfering with each other.

In general, a user's terminal can pay attention only to what is happening in one process at a time. This process is said to be in the *foreground*, and it communicates with the keyboard and the terminal screen. Other processes that may be running at the same time are called *background* processes. Background processes must be structured in such a way that they do not require access to the terminal. For example, results may be sent to a file, rather than to the terminal, then examined later at the user's convenience.

Unix Is a Multiuser System

Unix not only allows a single user to control multiple processes at once (multitasking), but also lets *multiple users,* each with a separate terminal, work on the system simultaneously. You can operate as if you "own" the system and all its resources are yours. You can also exchange messages and files with other users.

A *multiuser* system must restrict access to authorized users only. To maintain system security, users must log in with a preapproved user name and the correct secret password. Unix keeps track of who is using the system at any given moment, what each operator is doing, and what access privileges each operator has. In a single-user operating system such as DOS, however, there is no special provision for system security. It is simply assumed that unauthorized users will be denied physical access to the computer.

Since Unix is a *multiuser* operating system and DOS is not, the Unix features related to multiple-user operation have no counterparts in DOS. Each user on a multiuser system may be running several processes at any given moment. A computer running Unix, therefore, is generally working much harder than one running DOS. More of the system's capacity is used more of the time. As a result, more work can usually be accomplished with Unix. A disadvantage is that Unix systems tend to fail more often, since the hardware gets heavier use.

Unix Is More Flexible

One of the systematic differences between DOS and Unix is that a Unix command generally does only one thing. It may take two or more Unix commands to obtain the same result as from one DOS command. This structural difference makes Unix considerably more flexible than DOS. You can combine Unix commands in a great number of ways to produce precisely the results you want.

Finally, Unix is much larger and more robust than DOS. Unix not only contains more commands, but also includes a comprehensive set of software tools. These tools, designed to facilitate software development and text management, add a dimension to Unix that is missing from DOS and most other operating systems.

THE VERSIONS OF UNIX

Although the wide distribution and modification of Unix source code led to incompatibilities, Unix has remained remarkably consistent over the years. Only three versions have achieved widespread acceptance: System V, Berkeley Unix, and Xenix.

Unix System V Release 3.0

System V is the version of Unix that is officially endorsed and distributed by AT&T. Release 3.0 has gained widespread acceptance, and many of the nonofficial versions are migrating toward compatibility with it.

Berkeley Unix

Of all the universities that have had a hand in the development of Unix, none has had a greater influence than the University of California at Berkeley. The BSD versions developed at Berkeley introduced many of the features that are now important parts of System V. Even more BSD features will appear in future releases of System V.

Xenix

In 1981, AT&T licensed Unix System III to Microsoft Corporation, which distributed it under the name Xenix. Microsoft's target market, the microcomputer, was growing much faster than the minicomputer or mainframe market at that time. As a result, Xenix has been installed on more computers than any other version of Unix, although its market penetration is small compared to that of DOS.

Over the years, Microsoft has extended Xenix; currently it is much closer to System V than it is to the earlier System III. In addition, it includes many of the most important features of Berkeley Unix. Microsoft has turned over the marketing of Xenix to The Santa Cruz Operation, Inc. (SCO), which distributes versions for 8086-based, 80286-based, and 80386-based computers.

Unix System V Release 3.2

Release 3.2 represents a merging of Unix System V and Xenix System V, bringing together two of the three main branches of the Unix family tree. Interactive Systems

Corporation of Santa Monica, California distributes this product, as does SCO. It is available for 386 machines, but not for the less-powerful 86 and 286 computers.

Unix System V Release 4.0

System V release 4.0 (SVR4) is AT&T's candidate for a universally acceptable standard Unix. It merges the Sun-OS variant of the BSD Unix into the base formed by System V Release 3.2, thus creating a version that contains all the major features of System V, Berkeley Unix, and Xenix. In addition, Release 4.0 is designed to be used internationally. Biases toward the US-style representation of dates, times, and numbers have been removed. By progressively incorporating some of the best features of other versions, AT&T is trying to make System V a standard that will be acceptable to everyone.

In this book, we will use Xenix 2.3 and Unix System V Release 3.2 for our examples, since they are the primary precursors of SVR4. If you are using a different version, you may find slight differences.

User Interfaces

Since Unix was originally developed for use by computer experts, the user interface leaves much to be desired, from the viewpoint of the average computer user. Instead of choosing from menus, the user must enter command lines. Commands are cryptic, and syntax is not particularly consistent from one command to another. The newest releases are addressing this problem with a variety of graphically oriented user interfaces.

No single interface has yet emerged as dominant. The X Window System™ has received widespread support and forms the basis for many of the graphical-interface candidates. Sun's NeWS™ interface is popular because Sun hardware is so widespread. AT&T supports the OPEN LOOK™ interface, while the Open Software Foundation (OSF) advocates an interface named Motif™. These interfaces promise to make Unix accessible to ordinary mortals at last.

The examples in this book are not based on any one of these competing interfaces. We will use the traditional line-oriented command syntax.

SUMMARY

After growing slowly for two decades, the Unix operating system is currently experiencing widespread acceptance in the marketplace, thanks to the efforts of a small group of proponents at AT&T, at many universities, and at a number of minicomputer companies. Unix is the operating system of choice on engineering workstations and minicomputers. Penetration of the high-end personal-computer market is expanding rapidly. Personal computers based on the Intel 80286, 80386, and 80486 and on the Motorola 68020 and 68030 microprocessors all support one of the leading versions of Unix.

The primary personal-computer operating system, PC-DOS, has evolved over the years into a form that has much in common with Unix. DOS users will be able to apply much of their knowledge of that operating system to Unix. Much of the structure and many of the functions are the same in the two operating systems. There are, of course, differences in command syntax and other details, since no attempt was ever made to make the two operating systems compatible with each other. On the other hand, many of the general methods that have worked for you under DOS to generate a certain result will also work under Unix. In later chapters, examples of Unix commands will be given and compared to corresponding DOS commands.

However, since Unix is a richer and more complete operating environment, many of its features have no DOS equivalents. The additional Unix features represent new tools which will allow you to perform tasks more quickly, easily, and precisely than was possible with the DOS toolbox. The multiuser, multitasking capabilities of Unix will also be new to the DOS user.

Although several versions of Unix have been in use over the years, the most important recent versions are converging toward System V Release 4.0. There is now strong support for standardization of Unix.

A number of graphical interfaces are also competing to become the standard interface for making Unix more user-friendly.

Chapter 2

The Structure of Unix

This chapter identifies the parallels and contrasts between Unix and DOS, the operating system commonly used on personal computers. Unix is at least an order of magnitude more complex than DOS by virtue of its multiuser, multitasking, and virtual memory capabilities. The overall structure of Unix is described, providing a framework for the material presented in succeeding chapters.

THE PARTS OF AN OPERATING SYSTEM

An operating system is a layer of software that lies between the computer hardware and the application programs. Although operating systems can differ greatly, they all share certain common elements.

1. One part of the operating system controls essential operations, such as transferring data between main memory (RAM) and peripheral devices. This segment is itself resident in RAM; in Unix it is called the *kernel*.

2. The *file system* determines how files are organized on the mass-storage medium (usually disk).

3. The operating system must communicate with the user via the system terminal. In Unix, this user interface is called the *shell*.

4. Operating-system commands and programs that are needed less often than kernel commands may be stored on disk. They are called *utilities* in the Unix system.

THE PARTS OF DOS

DOS is a simple operating system that contains all four of the elements listed above. A major portion of DOS—the kernel—resides in RAM and controls basic system operation. The user can manipulate this kernel to some extent through *internal* commands, which reside in RAM at all times.

The DOS file system has a hierarchical tree-like structure that can accommodate thousands of files located in directories on one or more high-capacity hard disks.

The DOS user shell is contained in a file named **command.com.** The shell accepts input from the keyboard and other input devices and sends output to the terminal screen and other output devices.

External DOS commands correspond to Unix utilities. They perform functions that are needed frequently, but not often enough to justify leaving them in RAM all the time.

QNX is responsiable

proxy — доверенность
полномочия

interprocess com | Low level network com. | process scheduling | first level interrupt

msses proxies signals

THE PARTS OF UNIX

SIG

Like DOS, Unix incorporates the four major elements of an operating system. However, the Unix elements are, in general, much more elaborate than their DOS counterparts.

function

The Kernel

The kernel is the portion of Unix that resides in RAM and controls basic system operation. It allocates memory and disk storage, mediates the flow of data between memory and peripheral devices, handles interrupts and errors, schedules the running of processes, and responds to processes' requests for service.

function

1. Interrupt handler
2 system call
3 request for service.

1 *Operating Modes*

user mode
Kerner (after IRQ)

A single CPU can do only one thing at a time; it cannot run a user application while simultaneously executing kernel code. Thus, at any given moment, a Unix system is either in *user mode* running an application or in *kernel mode* executing an operating system function.

1

A system running in user mode tends to stay in user mode until an event occurs that switches execution to kernel mode. One event that can cause the switch is an *interrupt*. An interrupt is a low-level signal built into the hardware that causes execution to switch to a predefined software routine within the kernel called an *interrupt handler*. In a time-sharing operating system such as Unix, the system clock interrupts execution many times per second, allowing a switch from one application to another. Other kinds of interrupts may also occur. In every case, the kernel controls the switch.

② system call

A second event that will cause a switch from user mode to kernel mode is a *system call*. The system call is an application's way of communicating with the kernel. If an application needs to use a system resource or perform an operating system command, it issues a system call to the kernel. The kernel performs the desired service, then sends the result back to the application.

3 request for service

A third event that can cause a switch from user mode to kernel mode is a *request for service* by a peripheral device. Peripherals generally operate quite a bit more slowly than program execution in the CPU. Thus, the user program may be suspended for a large number of clock cycles while it awaits data from a peripheral device.

13

Kernel process

2 User Processes

active
suspended (standby) (blocked)

Under Unix, work is performed by *processes*. A process is a program in a state of execution. Thus, a user program becomes a process when it is running in the system.

At any given moment, a process is either *active* or *suspended*. The active process is the one running at the given moment. All other processes in the system are suspended. A suspended process is either *ready-to-run* or *blocked*. The highest-priority process that is ready to run will become the active process after the next time-slice interrupt. A blocked process must await an external event, such as the return of data from a peripheral device, before it is ready to run.

To insure that execution passes smoothly from one process to the next and that the highest-priority ready-to-run process is always selected, Unix stores process information in two tables: the *process table* and the *user table*. — *in format for active PS*

standby

The process table is always in memory. It contains one entry for each process. The entry includes the location of the process in memory or on the swap disk, the size of the process, and information about signals received by the process. This information must be available even when a process is suspended, because an event (such as the return of data from a peripheral) that occurs while a process is suspended may change its status from blocked to ready to run. The capacity of the process table determines the number of processes the system can support. If all entries in the table have been assigned, no additional processes can be launched.

Each process in the system has its own user table. The user table contains information that is needed only when the process is active; the user table may therefore be swapped out to disk. The kernel may access only the user table for the active process.

Basic Kernel Processes

PID

sched
Init
vhand
bdflush
—11—

0
1
2
3
4

In addition to user processes, the kernel has processes of its own. Some of these control the basic operation of the system. These basic processes are also called *demons*.

The first process to execute after a Unix system is booted is the *scheduler* (**sched**). It has a process ID (pid) of 0 and determines which of the ready-to-run processes on the system will execute next. The scheduler starts the *initialization process* (**init**).

(PID)
see PS

Init, which has a pid of 1, is responsible for keeping all other system demons running as they should. It makes sure the system is in the proper state of execution (multiuser, single-user, ready to power off, etc.). The **shutdown** command is one way of changing the init state of a system.

14

The *virtual handler process* (**vhand**) has a pid of 2. It manages the virtual memory, deciding which processes will remain in real memory and which will be swapped to disk. The virtual handler and the scheduler work closely together in controlling the system.

bdflush

The *buffer-to-disk flush* process (**bdflush**) and the *buffer-map flush* process (**bmapflus**) have pids of 3 and 4, respectively. They periodically flush the data in the system buffers out to disk. Since the buffers are volatile, they must be flushed to disk often. This protects the system from a mismatch between the data on disk and the corresponding data in system buffers if a system failure should occur.

These basic kernel processes are operational at all times and need not be || *VIP* requested by the user.

4 ## *Time Slicing*

Time sharing creates the illusion that each process running on a system has the system to itself. The system creates this illusion by sending an interrupt to the scheduler many times per second. At each interrupt, the current active process is suspended, and the highest-priority ready-to-run suspended process becomes active. This new active process then runs for a period called a *time slice* before itself being interrupted. Thus, although only one process is running at any given time, all processes in the system get their fair share of execution time.

5 ## *Swapping*

Unix is a *virtual-memory* operating system. This means it is possible to run multiple processes that collectively use more memory than is physically installed in the computer. To augment the system memory (random-access memory, or RAM), an area on disk is set aside called the *swap space*. This area may be used only for swapping and is not available for storing files.

When the memory requirements of the processes currently running exceed the amount of available RAM, the scheduler swaps out to disk the process that is least likely to be active again soon. Performance is optimized because the most active processes are retained in RAM, which is about 100,000 times faster than disk storage. When the time arrives for a swapped process to become active, it is swapped back into RAM and executed from there.

If your system RAM is insufficient for the memory requirements of your typical job mix, performance may be noticeably degraded due to excessive swapping. If this occurs, consider installing more RAM to reduce swapping.

When installing Unix, be sure to allocate enough swap space on your disk to accommodate the largest processing load you anticipate. If swap space fills up completely and another request for memory is received, your Unix system will probably crash.

The File System

The Unix file system is covered in chapter 7. Like the DOS file system, it is hierarchical, with paths linking directories in a tree structure. An extensive set of file-manipulation commands is available that goes well beyond the rather limited number of commands provided in DOS. Unix will allow you to perform all manipulations you are accustomed to performing with DOS, and quite a few more as well.

The Shell *(interprets cmnds for kernel)*

The shell is the interface between the user and the operating system. It interprets the commands typed at the terminal and translates them into terms understandable to the kernel. In DOS, the shell is not generally mentioned by name, but it is always executed when the system is booted. Additional copies of the DOS shell, **command.com,** may be launched by applications to allow their users to access DOS commands without exiting the application.

With Unix, three different shells are available. On systems that provide all three, you may use whichever you find most convenient. The oldest and most widespread is the *Bourne shell*. The *C shell* first appeared on Berkeley Unix and is also very popular. Finally, the *Korn shell* incorporates many of the best features of the Bourne and C shells, as well as some additional ones of its own. In this book, the Bourne shell syntax will be used in most cases. When a feature described is not available under the Bourne shell, the shell it does run under will be explicitly identified. Shell programming is explained in chapter 12.

Cmds — External 89% (Save on disc) / internal ≈11% (resident in RAM / memory)

Utilities

Under DOS, the majority of the operating system commands are internal; they are always resident in memory and form part of the kernel. The rest are external commands and are stored on disk until they are needed. In contrast, only a few of the Unix operating system commands are included in the kernel. Unix has over 300 commands (far more than DOS). Most of them are external to the kernel, residing on disk, and they are called utilities. Since Unix requires much more memory than does DOS, this arrangement saves RAM space, helping keep down memory requirements and system costs.

INTERPROCESS COMMUNICATION

ITC. In QNX is a part of microkernel.

Some applications may launch several processes, each working on a separate section of a single overall task. It may be helpful to send intermediate results from one such process to another during the course of execution. Unix provides several mechanisms for such information transfer, which will be discussed in chapter 10.

child parent fork signals.

TASK PROTECTION

As it is possible for one process to send information to another, then it is also possible for one process to damage another, either inadvertently or intentionally. To protect processes from damage, Unix maintains stringent controls over the types of communication permitted between them. Unix also prevents processes from accessing memory outside of their assigned areas, which is another possible cause of damage.

SUMMARY

The DOS and Unix operating systems are similar in that they both incorporate a kernel, a file system, a user shell, and a set of utilities or commands. Beyond that, differences are substantial.

The Unix kernel is much more complex than the DOS kernel, in order to control time sharing between multiple processes, multiuser operation, and virtual memory. The Unix file system, shells, and utilities are also more complex and more comprehensive than their DOS counterparts. Experience with DOS will help you understand Unix, but be prepared to deal with commands that are generally more complicated and more cryptic than DOS commands.

The essential structural difference between DOS and Unix is that DOS is a single-user, single-tasking system. Unix's time-sharing capability improves system efficiency, and its multiuser nature opens up possibilities that DOS lacks.

## Chapter 3

Hardware Considerations and System Installation

B efore a Unix operating system can be used, it must be installed on a computer. In the past, Unix users generally did not need to be concerned with installation because it involved modifying hardware in a mainframe or large multiuser minicomputer, and someone else took care of it. However, Unix is now running on many thousands of powerful microcomputers. Because these microcomputer-based systems are by far the fastest-growing segment of the Unix community, the role of the Unix user has changed. The personal Unix system is now a reality, as is the small work-group LAN system. A single user may wear multiple hats, including that of the installation technician and the system administrator. The first part of this chapter will discuss the components needed for a microcomputer-based Unix system and the criteria that should be applied when selecting them. The last part of the chapter addresses the process of installing and configuring the system.

SYSTEM HARDWARE

Unix is available on 80286 and 80386 machines, as well as on machines using the Motorola 68000 family of processors. More recently, implementations based on high-performance reduced instruction set computer (RISC) processors have become available from a variety of vendors at attractive prices. Although versions of Unix have been made to run on systems as small as an 8088-based IBM PC, they have been largely inadequate in both usefulness and speed.

This book is written for DOS users and is biased toward machines using the Intel 80X86 family of processors. However, most of the material in this chapter (as well as in the rest of the book) is indifferent to the details of the hardware configuration used, including the type of processor.

Processor Choice

The Intel 8086 and 286 do support Unix, but it would be a mistake to buy a machine based on either of those processors to run a multiuser, multitasking operating system. Architectural limitations of those chips restrict them to a low performance level.

On the other hand, a microcomputer based on the Intel 386 microprocessor makes an excellent platform for a small Unix system. Machines based on the inexpensive 386SX processor serve the purpose well for a *personal* system. Full-function 386 processors with clock speeds of 20 MHz and above can support *multiple users* comfortably. With a 386 machine, you can continue to run your existing DOS applications while building a library of Unix applications as well.

Be sure to get a version of Unix that was specifically designed to run on a 386 processor. Although Unix systems designed to run on a 286 will probably work on a 386 machine, they will not be able to take advantage of the 386's advanced features, and performance will be seriously handicapped.

The Intel 486 processor is functionally equivalent to the 386, but it offers more speed in a more thoroughly integrated package. All the advantages mentioned for the 386 apply to the 486 as well.

Computers based on the Motorola 68020, 68030, and 68040 microprocessors, as well as on various RISC chips, also make excellent Unix platforms. However, these machines are not capable of running DOS or OS/2. If you want one system that will run DOS (or OS/2) as well as Unix, you should choose a 386- or 486-based system.

System Memory

System memory, also known as *real memory* and *RAM*, is another vital part of any computer system. Unix, like OS/2, requires substantially more real memory than does the single-user, single-tasking DOS operating system. A bare-bones Unix system requires at least 2 megabytes of RAM to run even the most trivial applications. You may need even more to accommodate optional features such as network support and graphical user interfaces. More RAM may also be required to support a large number of simultaneous users.

Removable Storage Media

A Unix system, like any other system, requires a storage device with removable media. This device is used to load software onto the system and to remove data from the system. Typically, it is a floppy-disk drive or a cartridge-tape drive. In general, smaller systems have floppy-disk drives and larger systems have tape drives. Some systems have both.

Floppy disks, which usually have capacities of 1.2 megabytes and 1.44 megabytes, are a good choice for software loading if the package is not more than a few megabytes in size. For backup purposes, floppies are impractical if your data files will be larger than a few megabytes. Too much effort must be expended changing diskettes during the backup operation.

Tape cartridges have much larger capacities, varying between 60 megabytes and 150 megabytes, making them a practical backup medium. On larger Unix systems, software is also delivered on tape, making a floppy-disk drive unnecessary.

If you have an 80X86-based machine and intend to run DOS or OS/2 as well as Unix on it, you will need a floppy-disk drive for the non-Unix operating system. For most installations, it makes sense to have both a floppy-disk drive and a cartridge tape drive on your system.

On-Line Storage

The primary storage device on nearly all Unix systems is a high-performance hard disk. Ranging in capacity from 40 megabytes to over 1 gigabyte, these disks are the repository for all the system's programs and data. With average access times of from 10 to 30 milliseconds, hard disks are about 100,000 times slower than RAM. It makes sense to copy active programs and needed data from disk to RAM and operate on them in RAM. The less often your system must go to disk for data or program segments, the better its overall performance will be.

In general, hard disks are never big enough. A corollary of Parkinson's Law states that a computer system's program and data files grow to fill all available space. When computing how much hard-disk capacity you will need, add a healthy "fudge factor" to cover the unforeseen storage requirements that are bound to crop up. Always buy a larger hard disk than you think you will need.

Be sure the hard disk you buy for your Unix system is compatible with your hard-disk *controller.* In turn, the controller must be supported by a *device driver* that is compatible with your processor hardware and your Unix software. A device driver is a piece of software that interfaces your highly *generalized* Unix kernel to a highly *specific* peripheral device. In 80X86 machines, the characteristics (number of cylinders, heads, sectors, etc.) of the most common hard-disk drives are stored in ROM. The device driver for the hard disk uses this information to determine where on the disk each specific piece of information is located.

System Console

Every Unix system has a system console. The system console is the only place where the system administrator can log in as the root user and where boot-time messages and system-error messages are displayed. On large, older Unix systems, a slow printing terminal such as a Teletype machine was dedicated to this task. Most of the time, the system console sat idle. Today, it is common for the system console to be used as an ordinary terminal when it is not functioning as the system console. On a single-user system, it would clearly be a waste to dedicate a terminal solely to system-console duties. On small, informal multiuser systems, shared use of the system console is common. On larger systems, where the system administration load is greater, it is reasonable to dedicate one terminal as a full-time system console.

Remote Terminals and Serial Ports

Unix systems are designed to provide service to users through remote terminals, which may be quite distant from the computer and the system console. These remote terminals are connected to the computer via RS-232 serial ports. Modems, mice, and some types of printers also use serial ports to connect to their host computers. Your system must have enough such ports to support all the terminals and other peripheral devices you will be using.

Most 286 and 386 machines come with one serial port as standard equipment. Additional ports may be added as options; a wide variety of add-in boards are available for that purpose. Capacities range from one to 16 ports per board. If your computer has multiple expansion slots, it is relatively easy to provide ports for dozens of terminals.

Printers

A hardcopy device is a necessary part of any computer system. The most common such device is the printer. It is usually connected to the computer by a parallel port, but some models use a serial port instead.

The printer provides tangible output, which the user can more easily analyze, and a readable record of the computations carried out by the computer. Although you can attach more than one printer to a computer, one is usually sufficient.

A software device called the *spooler* allows multiple users to send files to the printer at the same time. The spooler buffers the output streams from the users and prints them sequentially. A print job does not start until the previous one is completed.

NETWORKING *(It is not nessesory multitask. OS)*

Multiuser systems and networked systems are often confused. Multiuser operation and networked operation are entirely different things. A multiuser system may or may not be hooked to a network. A network may or may not support multiuser operation.

In a multiuser system, two or more users, all with their own terminals, may simultaneously use a single processor. Unix is such a multiuser operating system. DOS and OS/2 are single-user systems. They can communicate with only one user, at a single terminal.

A network is a group of computers linked together to exchange information and share peripheral devices. Each processor on the network, called a *node,* can operate even if all the other nodes are turned off. If Unix is running on a network node, that node can support multiple users, each connected to the processor by an RS-232 serial port.

MINIMUM HARDWARE REQUIRED

A useful, low-cost Unix system that still delivers good performance for one or two users would contain a 386 microprocessor and 2 megabytes of memory. The system would also incorporate either a 1.2-megabyte 5.25-inch disk drive or a 1.44-megabyte 3.5-inch drive for software loading and backup. The system hard disk should have a capacity of at least 40 megabytes. The system's single serial port could be connected directly to a remote terminal or to a modem. If the port is connected to a modem, the second user could work at any location in the world that has a telephone. Connect a printer to the system's parallel port to round out the minimal configuration.

HARDWARE VERIFICATION

The hardware required for even a minimal system is fairly involved, and it is a sizable task to connect it all correctly. In addition, it is possible that one or more components of the system may be faulty. The Unix operating system is also large, complex, and potentially faulty. You should therefore check out the hardware configuration thoroughly before installing the Unix software. Then you know that any problems you encounter are unlikely to be hardware problems. They will be problems either with the software or with compatibility between the hardware and software.

One way to verify the integrity of your hardware is to install a small DOS partition on your hard disk and exercise the system thoroughly under DOS. If everything functions properly, you can install your Unix software.

HARD-DISK FORMATTING

Before you can put any software on a hard disk, the disk must be formatted. An unformatted disk cannot store data. There are two kinds of format operation: the low-level format and the high-level format.

When software documentation refers to formatting, it generally means the high-level format operation. This operation writes a pattern on the disk that allows it to accept data and reliably retrieve it. Formatting also detects flaws in the disk and maps around them. If a faulty sector is encountered, a substitute from a spare track on the disk is logically mapped onto its place. Thus, the logical memory space on the disk is unbroken, even though the physical memory space may be marred by numerous flaws. The software will never "see" those flawed spots.

The low-level format is generally performed by the hard-disk manufacturer, and, under normal circumstances, a user need not worry about it. However, if a disk's low-level format is ever disrupted, the only way to make the disk usable again is to perform a low-level format. The DOS debug utility can do a low-level format, as can other utilities on the market. Such a utility may be provided with your disk drive. If you are having disk problems that a high-level format does not clear up, try a low-level format before giving up on the disk. If it still does not respond, you may not be able to use it as anything except a bookend or doorstop.

UNIX SYSTEM INSTALLATION

The installation of one Unix variant may differ from the installation of another in the details, but certain elements are common to all. You must have permission to perform the software installation, and you must be logged in at the system console. These precautions prevent unauthorized users from disrupting the work of other users. The installation procedure is largely automatic; the user is prompted from time to time to make a decision that will affect system configuration.

The first step is to boot a minimal version of the Unix kernel from floppy disk. It first checks the hardware configuration to verify that enough system memory and hard-disk space are present, then gives you the opportunity to create a bootable Unix partition on your hard disk. The utility for doing this is usually called **fdisk**. If you already have a DOS partition on the disk, Unix allows you to place your Unix partition immediately above it. You can have up to four partitions on a disk, each with its own operating system. If the operating systems are incompatible, as are DOS and Unix, you will not be able to exchange files across the partition boundary.

The next step is a high-level format, which includes a stringent analysis of the recording surfaces of the disk platters. Any bad blocks are noted in a table and mapped around.

After the hard disk has been checked and formatted, file systems are installed. You are given the choice of creating either one or multiple file systems. For small Unix systems, it is generally best to create only one file system. With multiple file systems, you cannot copy files directly from one system to another.

The setup procedure includes allocation of space on your hard disk for a swap area. Swap space is needed because Unix supports virtual memory.

If your Unix system has 2 megabytes of real memory, virtual memory allows you to run several tasks simultaneously, even though the tasks collectively take up more than 2 megabytes. What does not fit in real memory is stored in virtual memory. Logically, virtual memory seems to be an extension of real memory. In actuality, however, it is the swap space on the disk.

Virtual memory works on the principle that, even though a program is active, not all its program code and data are needed all the time. The portions of a task that are active at a given moment are kept in real memory, while those that are not are swapped out to disk. When the inactive portions are needed, they will be swapped back in and something else will be swapped out. Thus, a system with 2 megabytes of real memory and 2 megabytes of swap area on disk runs almost as fast as a system with 4 megabytes of real memory. When swaps take place too frequently, however (a condition known as *thrashing*), performance will be seriously degraded. If thrashing begins to happen often, it is time to add more real memory to your system.

During installation, when you are asked how much space to allocate for the swap area, be sure to allocate plenty. During operation, if applications try to use more memory than is available, the system will crash. Much valuable work could be lost. Calculate the maximum memory requirements of applications likely to be run on your system and set your swap space allocation accordingly. If the ratio of virtual memory to real memory is too high, your system will slow down noticeably. This is a nuisance, but preferable to a system crash.

Once the installation of the base system is complete, give it a thorough workout before adding optional software packages or application programs. An operating-system fault is much simpler to isolate and identify if it is not obscured by an intervening layer of application code.

Installing Optional Packages

As is the case with installing the base-system packages, you must have permission to execute the privileged operations that install or remove optional software. You must also be logged in at the system console.

The system add-on installation procedure is largely automatic. If the new system was delivered on multiple floppy disks, you will be prompted to mount each one in turn. Before installation begins, your hard disk will be automatically checked to make sure you have enough space available to hold the new software. If there is insufficient space, you will be prompted to remove some existing files before attempting to install the software again.

Removal of software systems is also automatic. This assures that all files associated with a system are removed, so your hard disk does not become cluttered with the remnants of obsolete software packages.

Optimizing the System Configuration

After your system is installed, determine your users' needs in terms of storage and computational resources. If your users need a lot of disk space for their files, but relatively little RAM during operation, you may be able to decrease the amount of disk space allocated to the swap area and free it up for file storage. On the other hand, heavy use of the virtual-storage facility may justify adding additional real memory to improve performance.

A single, low-speed impact printer may be sufficient for a modest printing load, if instant turnaround of print jobs is not a requirement. For installations where printing is critical, you may want to install two or more high-speed printers to improve job turnaround time.

Another item you can adjust based on experience is the number of modems attached to the system. If the number of remote users attempting to log in frequently exceeds the number of modems available, you may want to add additional modems to improve the availability of your system to remote clients.

SUMMARY

Unix, a multiuser, multitasking operating system, requires significantly more resources than does DOS. For acceptable performance, the base microprocessor should be at least an 80386- or 68020-class chip. Minimum real-memory size is 2 megabytes, and the system hard disk should have a capacity of at least 40 megabytes.

Remote terminals, as well as modems, mice, and some types of printers, are connected to the system by RS-232 serial ports. When buying a system, consider how many serial ports you might need to add as your system expands.

Install your system in a step-by-step fashion, stopping to verify each step before proceeding to the next. A fully operational Unix system is a very complex combination of hardware, system software, and application software. It is much easier to track down a problem if you can isolate it to just one of these specific areas.

If you are installing Unix on your hard disk along with one or more other operating systems, be sure to allocate enough space for the Unix system software, application programs, and data. In addition, you will need to reserve generous space for a swap area.

If, after loading all your software onto hard disk, you find that the amount of free space is ominously low, you may want to add a second hard disk to your configuration. Alternatively, you can replace your existing hard disk with a larger one and reload your software.

As your processing load goes up, add more RAM if your system slows down too much. This will transfer processing from virtual memory into the faster real memory.

Chapter 4

Using Disks with Unix

U nix systems, like most computers, incorporate two kinds of read-write memory: *system memory* and *on-line storage*. System memory, also called RAM, is very fast, but is relatively small and volatile. When power to a computer system is interrupted or removed, all information stored in volatile memory is lost. On-line storage is about 100,000 times slower, but is relatively large and nonvolatile. When power to a computer system is interrupted, all information stored in volatile memory is lost. Nonvolatile memory, however, retains its information when the machine is turned off. A typical Unix system has several megabytes of system memory and may have up to several hundred megabytes of on-line storage.

This chapter will focus on the most common form of on-line storage, the hard disk. It will also discuss the floppy disk, which is the common medium for exchanging programs and data between systems.

BLOCKS VS. BYTES

DOS users are accustomed to thinking of file and disk sizes in terms of bytes. Unix normally deals with blocks rather than bytes. There are two types of blocks in the Unix storage system, *physical* and *logical*. A physical block is a portion of a track on disk and is 512 bytes long. A logical block is a portion of a file and is some standard length, usually 1024 bytes. A logical block is not necessarily identified with a single location on a disk. Commands that return values to you in terms of blocks are referring to physical blocks.

INODES *(in DOS FAT—File Location Table)*

Every file in a file system is associated with an *inode*, or identification node. Since the Unix file system may scatter pieces of a file throughout the system disk, particularly if the disk is highly fragmented, there must be a mechanism to keep track of all the pieces. The inode is that mechanism. Each inode contains information about its associated file's location on disk, as well as the file's length, access modes, last modification date, and owner. A table of inodes is located near the top of each file system. The inode table performs the same function for Unix that the file allocation table (FAT) performs for DOS. If the inode table is damaged, you may be unable to access some or all of the files in the associated file system. The number of files in a file system may not exceed the number of inodes.

inodes — most critical part of disk and need to be protected

FILE SYSTEMS AND PHYSICAL DISKS

A file system is a hierarchical directory structure containing related files. Since a hard disk may have a capacity of hundreds of megabytes, several unrelated file systems may be stored on one disk. The converse, however, is not true. Unix does not allow a single file system to span two hard disks. A file system must be completely contained on a single disk device.

30

HARD DISK MANAGEMENT

It is important to maintain the integrity of the file systems on your hard disk. This becomes critical as a large hard disk begins to fill up. If you try to pack more data on a disk than it can hold, problems are bound to occur. You may lose valuable information.

Determining the Amount of Free Disk Space

Under DOS, to see how much space is available on your disk, you use the **dir** command. It will list the names, sizes, and creation dates of the files in the current directory, then display the number of bytes of unused space.

Under Unix, you use the **df** (disk free) command to determine how much disk space is available. It will return to you the number of blocks (not bytes) of space available on all mounted file systems:

```
$ df
/          (/dev/root )>:      31114 blocks      5104 inodes
$
```

The **df** command will not list the files in the current directory; it will only tell you the total number of unused blocks and unused inodes in the mounted file systems. If you specify a file system name, it will give you the number of unused blocks in that file system.

To see what percentage of the entire system storage is used, specify the **-v** option:

```
$ df -v
Mount Dir   Filesystem    blocks      used      free     used
/           /dev/root     50638      19522     31116      39%
$
```

If the free space in your file system is less than 15% of the total capacity of the disk, it is time to remove unneeded files. System performance starts to degrade noticeably when free space gets low.

Determining Amount of Disk Space Already Used

The Unix **du** (disk usage) command corresponds to the other function of the DOS **dir** command. It lists the name of each subdirectory (or, if desired, each file) in the current directory, along with the number of blocks that it occupies. (Directories are discussed in chapter 7.) You can specify a directory (including its subdirectories) other than the current one, if you wish. Various options are available that specify the level of detail of the output. The default display includes only the current directory, its subdirectories, and the number of blocks of storage used in each:

In the following example, there are 1874 blocks in use in the vpix directory and its subdirectories, which translates to 1874 by 512 bytes, or 959 kilobytes:

```
$ pwd
/usr/vpix
$ du
218        ./bin
536        ./defaults
984        ./dosbin
66         ./term
10         ./xenixbin
1874       .
$
```

Show your location

Flushing the Buffers

The Unix file system, like the DOS file system, is very flexible in the allocation of disk space. It is not necessary to set aside a predetermined space on disk before writing a file. Furthermore, existing files can grow as large as desired, limited only by the capacity of the disk. This flexibility is made possible by an indirect method of addressing files. Since indirect addressing can slow retrieval from disk, Unix supports the use of *disk buffers* to improve disk performance.

Unix has disk buffer (RAM)

Buffers are sections of main memory that are set aside to hold copies of information on disk. When the system asks for a disk block that is also in a buffer, Unix retrieves it from the buffer, rather than going out to disk for it. The result is a tremendous increase in speed, since system memory is orders of magnitude faster than disk memory. Similarly, if a program tries to write information to a disk block that is also in a buffer, the buffer is written, rather than the disk. Once again, performance increases dramatically.

However, there is also a danger. If the contents of a buffer have been changed and the corresponding disk block has not, the two storage areas are said to be *unsynchronized*. If operation were interrupted by a power-line transient, if someone shut off the computer, or if some other problem occurred, the discrepancy between the disk and the buffer would not be corrected. Files could be corrupted and data lost.

Sync restore synchron. between RAM buffer and Disk.

To restore synchronization, flush the buffers out to disk with the **sync** command before performing any risky operation that might cause a system crash. In fact, it is a good idea to run **sync** regularly. Many system administrators set up a background process that automatically runs **sync** every minute. If a crash occurs, only those files that have been changed within the previous minute are affected.

The correct way to turn off a Unix system is to use the **shutdown** command. Only the system administrator may issue this command, which usually resides in the **/etc** directory. Using the **shutdown** command is important because it calls the **sync** command to flush all buffers to disk. Only after **shutdown** action is complete can the power safely be removed from the system.

Sooner or later, all file systems become corrupted, despite the precautions you may take. When the inevitable occurs, the system administrator can often salvage some or all of the damaged files. Chapter 5 contains a discussion about recovering information from damaged files and disks.

FLOPPY-DISK MANAGEMENT

Floppy disks are a common medium for exchanging data between Unix systems, just as they are for DOS systems. Although the media and the disk drives on Unix systems are physically the same as those on DOS systems, one system cannot read a diskette that was written on the other. The formats are incompatible. You will have to reformat DOS diskettes before using under Unix. (In this book, floppy disk and diskette are used interchangeably.)

Use the Unix **format** command to format diskettes. The syntax is somewhat different from that of the DOS **format** command. To format the first 1.2-megabyte drive on the system, enter:

```
$ format /dev/rfd096ds15
```

If this drive is the default drive listed in **/etc/default/format**, you can use the simpler default device specification:

```
$ format /dev/rfd0
```

Unix will prompt you to insert a diskette; after doing so, press return. As it formats the diskette, the **format** command will display a running account of the track and head location of the area currently being formatted. Various options allow you to choose what is displayed during this process and whether the system will verify the diskette after formatting.

Putting a File System on a Diskette

After a diskette has been formatted, a file system must be placed on it before the diskette can be used. Only the system administrator, logged in as **root**, can create a file system. The system administrator's prompt is # rather than $.

Putting a file system on a diskette is not the same for Xenix as it is for Unix System V Release 3.2 (SVR3.2). For Xenix, after logging in as **root**, the system administrator places a formatted floppy into the A drive and issues the command:

```
# mkdev fd
```

The following menu will be displayed:

```
Choices for type of floppy filesystem.

1. 48 tpi, double sided, 9 sectors per track
2. 96 tpi, double sided, 15 sectors per track
3. 135 tpi, double sided, 9 sectors per track (3.5" diskette)

Enter an option or enter q to quit:
```

If you have a high-density 5.25-inch floppy drive and diskette, enter 2. The system will then prompt you to insert a diskette:

```
Insert a 96 tpi floppy into drive 0. Press Return to continue.
```

After you have inserted a formatted diskette, press [Return]. Another menu will appear:

```
Choices for contents of floppy filesystem.

1. Filesystem only
2. Bootable only
3. Root filesystem only
4. Root and Boot (only available for 96 tpi floppy)

Enter an option or enter q to quit:
```

For this example, select 1 and press [Return]. The system, using the **fdinit** command, will create a file system and report completion with the message:

```
96 tpi filesystem floppy complete.
```

With Unix SVR3.2, the **mkdev** command is not available. Instead, use **mkfs** combined with **labelit.** To create a file system on a 1.2-megabyte diskette, issue the command:

```
# /etc/mkfs /dev/dsk/f0q15d 2370:592 2 30
```

This will create a filesystem with 2370 blocks and 592 inodes. The rotational gap is 2, and there are 30 blocks per cylinder. Now give the file system a name with the **labelit** command:

```
# /etc/labelit /dev/dsk/f0q15d letter let2
```

The name of the file system is "letter" and the name of this volume is "let2." The file system name and volume name are restricted to a maximum of six characters.

Mounting and Unmounting Diskettes

Even after a filesystem has been created on a diskette, Unix still does not recognize the file system's presence. The file system on the diskette must be mounted onto the file system you are currently using. The **mount** command grafts the diskette's file system onto the active file system. The root directory has a subdirectory named **/mnt,** which is the normal place for mounting a removable storage device such as a floppy disk. You are not restricted to using **/mnt**, however. You may mount your floppy anywhere you wish in the directory tree. In most cases, though, you will probably want to use the **/mnt** directory, to maintain consistency with other Unix systems.

To mount a diskette installed in your 5.25-inch 1.2-megabyte drive, enter the command:

```
mount /dev/dsk/f0q15d /mnt
```

If you have a diskette mounted, it must be unmounted before you can issue the **shutdown** command to prepare the system to be powered down. Use the **umount** command, the syntax of which is:

```
umount /dev/dsk/f0q15d
```

Raw Access

It is possible to use diskettes and tapes without making them part of the active filesystem. Accessing a diskette without first adding a file system to it and mounting it is called *raw access.* Raw access is used primarily for backup and archiving, and also for transporting files from one Unix system to another. In general, the file systems of different Unix systems are mutually incompatible. Chapter 5 explores the various methods of backing up a Unix system. After a backup has been made, a filesystem can later be restored to the original system or to a different system.

Booting from Floppy Disk

Although you will normally boot your system from the hard disk, there may be occasions when you want or need to boot from floppy. For example, if your system administrator left the company and neglected to tell anyone the root password, you would lose control of the system. One solution would be to boot the system from a floppy and then mount the hard disk onto the floppy system. At that point, you could edit the password file to replace the old root password with a new one.

It is a good idea to make an emergency-boot floppy to provide insurance against such problems. To do so with Xenix, use the **mkdev fd** command (see "Putting a Filesystem on a Diskette" in this chapter). From the menu of choices for contents of floppy filesystem, select either **2. Bootable only** or **4. Boot and Root.** The diskette thus created can access your hard disk files if the normal hard disk filesystem is not operating properly.

MOVING FILES BETWEEN DISKS

Unix has several commands for copying data to and from disks and diskettes. Which command is best depends on whether you are copying single files or entire directories.

The cp Command

For copying one file or a small group of files from one active disk to another, **cp** is probably the best choice. To copy from a hard disk to a diskette, the diskette must be formatted, must have a filesystem on it, and must be mounted into the active file system. For example, to copy a file named **test** from the current directory to the mounted diskette, use the command:

```
cp test /mnt
```

The first argument (**test**) is the source file. The second argument (**/mnt**) is the destination directory. You can change the name of the copied file by specifying a different name for the destination file. For example, to change the name of the copied file from **test** to **oldtest**, use:

```
cp test /mnt/oldtest
```

The copy Command

The **copy** command is a superset of **cp** that is useful for copying entire directories to a disk. If the source argument is a directory, its contents are copied into the destination directory. If either the source or the destination is anything other than a directory, **copy** acts exactly like **cp**.

A number of options are available for the **copy** command. For example, the **-r** option *VIP* causes all subdirectories of the specified directory to be recursively copied as well. If the **-r** option is chosen, all the files in the source directory are copied to the destination. All files in all its subdirectories are also copied. The system will go down as many levels as necessary to make sure that all files in all subdirectories have been copied to the destination disk. Thus the command:

```
copy /usr/allen /mnt
```

copies all files in the directory **/usr/allen** to the mounted floppy disk, while the subdirectories of **/usr/allen** are ignored. However, the command:

```
copy -r /usr/allen /mnt
```

copies all files in **/usr/allen**, as well as all files in all its subdirectories, to the mounted floppy disk. Subdirectories are created on the destination disk that correspond exactly to the subdirectories on the source disk.

The cpio Command *(Row Access)*

The **cpio** command is an archiving command, more like the DOS **backup/restore** pair than like the DOS **copy** command. It requires that the destination disk be formatted, but does not require that a filesystem be present. The **cpio** command uses an archival format that is incompatible with the normal Unix filesystem. Consequently, you must refer to disk or tape drives by their raw device names when using it. Normal device names work only when a Unix file system is present. Chapter 5 discusses the use of **cpio** as a hard-disk-backup command.

where is floppy

The dd Command

Although the **dd** command can be used for copying files from one disk to another, its primary purpose is to convert files from one format to another. For instance, **dd** can be used to convert an EBCDIC file to ASCII or vice versa. It can also be used to convert a file containing both upper- and lowercase characters to all uppercase or all lowercase. The **dd** command also allows you to skip a specified number of records at the beginning of the source file before commencing the copy operation. In most cases, however, you will use **cp**, **copy**, or **cpio** to copy from one disk to another.

SUMMARY

disk usage

In Unix, disk space is divided into 512-byte blocks. Space is allocated into file systems. Every file in a file system is identified and located on the disk by the file's inode.

In many ways, hard-disk management in a Unix system is similar to hard-disk management in a DOS system. The Unix **df** and **du** commands can be used to determine the amount of unused disk space, much like the **dir** command is used in DOS. There are also substantial differences between the two operating systems. Unix makes far more extensive use of RAM buffers than does DOS. As a result, the danger of file corruption due to lack of synchronization between the buffers and the hard disk is far greater in Unix. To compensate for this potential weakness, Unix offers the **sync** command to allow you to synchronize buffers with disk whenever you want to.

command sync

Floppy-disk management is more tedious in Unix than in DOS because of the need to create file systems and to mount and unmount diskettes. The simpler DOS operating system has no such requirements. You can create a boot floppy under Unix in much the same way that a bootable DOS diskette is created.

Copying Unix files between hard disks and diskettes is similar to copying in DOS. The function of the Unix **cp** command is similar to that of the DOS **copy** command. The Unix **copy** command is considerably more powerful. It can copy entire directories, including subdirectories, from one disk to another. The **cpio** and **dd** commands can also be used for copying files, but their primary applications are in archiving and in format conversion, respectively.

Chapter 5

Hard-Disk Backup and Restoration

The vital importance of regularly backing up disk files is clearly understood by the directors of corporate management information systems (MIS) departments. But most people who run DOS on PCs do not take backup seriously enough. Many do not even bother to back up their work at all, and so far may not have suffered for their neglect.

Under Unix, the risk of data loss is higher, and the consequences more serious. Unix uses virtual memory to allow multiple processes to run simultaneously, even if RAM is not large enough to hold them all. Only the processes that are active at a given moment need to be in RAM. The others, which may be waiting for a response from a printer or other device, are swapped out to the hard disk. Consequently, a multiuser, multitasking Unix system uses its disk much more heavily than a DOS system does. The added wear and tear caused by the Unix system will probably cause the disk drive to fail sooner.

The most common cause of data loss is human error. This problem, along with losses caused by power surges and other kinds of accidental damage, can happen with even the most reliable disk drive. In a multiuser system, where many people depend on the availability and accuracy of the data they have entrusted to the hard disk, a strictly observed, formal backup procedure is absolutely essential. As a general rule, if information is being written to the system disk every day, then a backup should also be made every day.

Most users can logically divide the information stored on their hard disk into programs and data. Programs rarely change; once they have been backed up, they need not be backed up again unless they have been modified. Data files, however, must be backed up regularly.

TYPES OF BACKUP

There are several types of backup: full, incremental, and personal. Which backup method to use, and when to use it, depends on the extent of changes made to your disk files during normal activity.

Full Backup

The simplest method is *full backup*. Everything stored on the system hard disk is copied onto the backup medium, and you are assured of protection for all your data. Performing a full backup, however, can be so time-consuming and tedious that people may start finding excuses not to do it, thus leaving their data vulnerable to loss. In most cases, however, a full backup is not necessary.

Incremental Backup

After one full backup has been made, the next backup need archive only those files that have changed since. This partial backup is called an *incremental backup*.

Because Unix keeps track of when each file was created or last changed, it knows whether a file has been altered since the last backup. If a file was altered, the incremental backup procedure backs it up again. If not, it is skipped and the next file is examined.

If you should ever suffer a catastrophic loss of data, go back to your last full backup and restore it to the system first. Next, restore all incremental backups you have made since. The result will be a file system every bit as accurate as if it had been archived with a full backup every day.

The advantage of incremental backups is that they can be made much more quickly than full backups. The disadvantage is that they take more time and effort to restore. Since most systems are quite reliable, you will be performing the backup operation far more often than the restore operation. So making one full backup, followed by a series of incremental backups, is more efficient than performing a full backup every day.

Personal Backup

One of the system administrator's primary responsibilities is making sure that an adequate backup regimen is strictly followed. Even if this is the case, if you as a user have the resources to perform backups of your own files, it would be wise to do so.

Backing up your own files is a cheap form of insurance. It does not take too much time; you can even do backup as a background process (see chapter 10) while working on something else. The only requirement is that you have at your disposal a removable-media device, such as a floppy-disk drive or a cartridge-tape drive.

At the end of each work session, copy the files that have been modified to a backup disk or tape. Maintain several backup disks, and alternate them. Never back up to the same disk twice in a row. If a system failure should occur during the backup operation, you could lose the information on your backup disk, as well as that on your hard disk. Some users maintain a different backup disk for each day of the week. In most cases, however, alternating among three disks provides an adequate level of safety.

BACKUP MEDIA

There are several forms of backup media: tape cartridge, floppy disk, removable hard disk, and optical disk. Each medium is suited for particular backup needs. The characteristics of the data to be backed up or archived will determine which medium is best in any specific case.

Tape Cartridges as a Backup Medium

Magnetic tape has been used as a backup medium since the early days of computers. Tape cartridges today are basically the same as the tape reels used on the early mainframes, but they pack the data into a much smaller space.

Tape is a *serial-access* medium. If the read-write head of your tape drive is at one end of the tape, and the data you want is at the other, you must wind through the entire tape before you can start reading. For backup purposes, this is not a disadvantage. In restoring specific information from the tape to the hard disk, however, it may take you some time to reach the file you want.

Tape cartridges have much larger capacities than floppy disks (60 megabytes and more is common), so tape backup is preferable when you are dealing with multiple megabytes. If at all possible, you want to perform your entire backup without having to change the backup medium.

Floppy Disks as a Backup Medium

Floppy disks are *random-access* devices, in contrast to serial-access tapes. Information can be accessed directly and thus retrieved quickly, no matter where it is located on the disk. They are also more convenient and less expensive than tape cartridges.

Floppy disks are best for backing up relatively small amounts of information. The most commonly used floppy disks have capacities of 1.2 megabytes and 1.44 megabytes. If you are backing up less than that, floppies are practical. But if you have modified files that add up to more than 1 megabyte during a work session, you should not use floppies for backup. Instead, use tape, removable hard disks, or optical disks.

Removable Hard Disks as a Backup Medium

Until recently, tapes and floppy disks were the only removable media available on personal-computer systems and workstations. Now there is a wider range of choices, including *removable hard disks*.

These devices come in several forms and generally have capacities of 20 to 44 megabytes. With some, only the medium is removable, and the head/disk assembly remains in the computer. In others, the entire drive mechanism is removable. A removable hard disk can be used as a backup device in conjunction with a fixed disk that is permanently installed in the computer.

Optical Disks as a Backup Medium

Another form of removable storage is the *optical disk,* of which there are three types: *read-only, read/write*, and *write-once/read-many.*

A read-only optical disk (CD-ROM) is not a backup medium. Once it leaves the factory, a CD-ROM disk cannot be written on; that is why it is called read-only memory.

A read/write optical disk is functionally the same as a removable hard disk. However, it stores information optically, rather than magnetically. Optical disks have capacities comparable to the largest nonremovable hard disks, but they operate somewhat more slowly. They are practical for storing large quantities of information that is not needed often.

Write-once/read-many (WORM) optical disks can be written by the user, but only one time. Once information has been written to a WORM disk, it is *permanently* stored on the disk. This characteristic makes WORM media ideal for archiving information that is no longer in active use but that must be kept for possible later retrieval. WORM is also useful as a backup medium because it provides a permanent record of the evolution of a program or database, maintaining an audit trail of the progress of a development effort.

BACKUP COMMAND OPTIONS

Unix has several commands for performing backup, each with a somewhat different function. Which one you should use depends on the type of backup you are doing, the backup device you are using, and the nature of the files involved.

The backup (dump) Command

The **backup** command, called **dump** in some versions of Unix, can be used for both full and incremental backups. With arguments, you can specify which files will be backed up and which device they will be copied to. Individual files or entire file systems can be backed up.

The **backup** command is the best one for normal, everyday, working backup. Although it is designed to support incremental backups, it works equally well in making full backups.

It is possible to back up files that are collectively larger than the capacity of the backup medium you are using. This is accomplished through prompts that tell you to insert a new diskette or mount a new tape as the backup device becomes filled. If you are backing up to diskette, you must be sure that you have enough formatted diskettes on hand to hold the entire backup. Once the backup process is started, the system copies files to one diskette after another, prompting you to insert a new diskette as each one is filled. If you run out of formatted diskettes before you run out of data, the backup operation cannot be completed.

When backing up to tape, the same caution applies. Be sure you have enough formatted tapes on hand to hold the entire backup. When one tape is filled, the system will prompt you to mount another.

When a **backup** command is successfully completed, the date is recorded in the backup-log file **/etc/ddate**. This date is used by subsequent incremental backups to determine which files have been changed since the last backup and thus need to be backed up again.

In the **backup** command, you may specify a level from 0 to 9. The lowest level, 0, signifies a full backup. The highest level, 9, performs the incremental backup you should do every day. A level-9 backup copies only files that have changed since the last level-9 backup. If you do only level-9 backups, you will soon have an unwieldy number of backup disks or tapes to maintain. To prevent this problem, do a full or intermediate-level backup periodically. A level-8 backup, for example, will copy all files that have changed since the last level-8 backup. Then all diskettes that have been holding level-9 backups can be recycled.

The amount of data that you have to back up and the frequency with which it changes will determine whether it makes sense for you to use incremental backups. For small file systems, it is easiest to make a full backup every day. Since you can write a script to perform backup during an idle period, or when no operator is present, it may be practical to perform a full backup every day even if your file system is large. When performing an unattended backup, however, be sure your backup medium is large enough to hold everything. Otherwise, a human operator must be present to change volumes in response to a prompt.

The restore Command

Like the DOS **backup** command, the Unix **backup** command stores data in a format different from that of ordinary files. Therefore, backup files cannot be read and used directly. You must use the **restore** command to copy files from your backup medium into the system hard disk. This process converts the backup archive format to the ordinary Unix file format.

The cpio Command

The **cpio** command is a good one for personal backups and for archiving information you are unlikely to need again soon. Instead of copying each file individually, it copies all specified files to one large, compact archive file. This is particularly convenient when dealing with a large number of small files. The files remain individually retrievable, however, since information about their original file names is retained.

For example, to save all the files in the current directory to a formatted diskette in your default floppy drive, use the command:

```
ls | cpio -o > /dev/fd0
```

The file list created by the **ls** command is piped to the **cpio** command, which uses it as an input file list. The output of **cpio** is then redirected to the floppy drive specified by **/dev/fd0**. Piping and redirection are discussed in Chapter 7.

The **backup** command only backs up data, requiring the **restore** command to retrieve it. The **cpio** command can perform either function, depending on which argument is used with it. When used with the **-o** (output) option, **cpio** copies data from the system disk to an external storage device. The **-i** (input) option retrieves data from an external storage device to the system disk.

To retrieve the files written to diskette in the previous example, use the syntax:

```
cpio -i < /dev/fd0
```

This command directs the system to retrieve all files archived on device **fd0**.

The find Command

You can use the **find** command to select files that have been altered since the last backup. This is a convenient command to use for performing an incremental backup. After selecting files for incremental backup with **find**, you then use **cpio** to copy them to the backup medium.

The tar Command

The **tar** command, short for "tape archive," can be used with floppy disks as well as with tape. Since **tar** is common to a wide variety of Unix versions, it is often used to archive files for transport from one Unix system to another.

The function of **tar** is similar to that of **cpio**, but several options, or keys, are available. Depending on the key specified, **tar** will either create a new archive, add files to an existing archive, or extract files from an existing one.

Like the **cpio** command, **tar** is bidirectional. Unless you specify otherwise, tar will send files to the default archive device. The identity of this default device is stored in a file named **/etc/default/tar.**

For a Xenix system, the default is:

```
archive=/dev/rfd096ds15  10  1200  n
```

Here, the device is a 1.2-megabyte floppy-disk drive. The **n** indicates that the device is not a tape drive. A **y** in the same position would indicate that the default **tar** device is a tape drive. You may specify the output device in the **tar** command, thus overriding the default.

The following command copies all the files in the current directory that start with the letter t to the default **tar** device specified in **/etc/default/tar:**

```
tar cv t*
```

The following command lists the names of all the files currently stored on the default **tar** device:

```
tar t
```

Finally, the following command extracts all the files stored on the default **tar** device and copies them to the current directory of the system disk:

```
tar x
```

With the **tar** command, you can specify individual files, groups of files within a directory, all files in a directory, or all files in several directories, including their subdirectories. Thus, if you are backing up files scattered across several related directories, **tar** may be your best choice.

ORGANIZING DIRECTORIES FOR EASY BACKUP

You should make personal backups even though the system administrator maintains system integrity through a combination of full and incremental backups. During a single work session, you might make changes to files from several different applications. It may be difficult to remember which files should be included in an end-of-session personal backup. To avoid this problem, put all the files you are likely to modify during a work session into a single directory or group of related directories. Then you can easily back up the entire directory (or group of directories) with a single command. This procedure may back up some files that have not changed, but that will cause no harm. The time you save by not having to enter multiple commands should more than compensate for the extra time the computer takes to perform the actual backup operation.

ENFORCING A BACKUP DISCIPLINE

Whichever command or combination of commands you decide to use, be consistent about performing backup. The specific form of the backup is less important than performing it regularly, without fail. Since backups have no function in everyday operation, it is all too easy to skip them when time is short and other, seemingly more important, matters demand your attentions. However, the consequences of not having proper backup if you lose data on your main disk are potentially catastrophic.

Establish a formal backup procedure for all systems in your organization, that is always to be carried out as scheduled, no matter what else is happening. Make sure that one person is responsible for seeing that the backup is done. Designate an alternate to perform the backup when the regular person cannot.

One way to make the backup job easier, and thus less likely to be skipped, is to write a shell script with a series of backup commands. This series of commands will automatically back up all directories that are volatile (changing frequently). Once the script has started executing, you need pay no further attention to the operation until the backup is complete. At that point, just remove the backup medium, label it properly, and put it in a safe place.

Part of the backup discipline should be the periodic removal of backups to an off-site storage location. Having backup disks or tapes on-site will protect you against machine failures, but not against fires, floods, and other physical disasters.

Try to anticipate possible threats to your data, and devise procedures to avoid damage. The frequency with which you do backups should depend on how much work you can afford to lose in the event of a disk failure. In many cases, backing up once a day is enough. In some situations, however, more frequent backups are necessary. You must decide what is appropriate in your case.

UPGRADING HARD DISKS TO A NEW VERSION OF UNIX

The details of how to upgrade from one version of Unix to another will vary depending on the vendor of your particular copy. Follow the instructions that came with your operating system and with the upgrade. However, some general principles apply, regardless of which brand of Unix you are using.

Upgrades differ greatly in scope. A major update, such as that from Release 3.0 to Release 4.0, affects practically everything. On the other hand, a minor update may affect the root file system slightly and the user file systems not at all. The extent of the update determines how much work you will have to do and how long it will take. A major update may require that you format your hard disk and start from scratch.

Before installing any upgrade, perform a complete backup of your system. If for any reason the upgrade is unsuccessful, you will be able to reinstall your old system. For this backup, use the **tar** command. You must be logged in as the superuser in single-user mode to perform this backup. The backup should be the last operation performed before shutting down to install the upgrade. If other users are active while the backup is being performed, their files may be corrupted.

If you have any special device drivers that were not part of your original operating system, you will have to relink them to the upgraded system's kernel. After installing the new version, restore the files that you backed up, taking care not to restore old system files over the top of new ones from the new release. They may not be compatible.

For a major upgrade, even your old application programs may not work; new versions may be needed. In most cases, old applications can be made compatible with a new Unix version by recompiling them. A few applications may require more elaborate measures. However, your data files and text files should be all right as they are.

RECOVERING INFORMATION FROM DAMAGED FILES AND DISKS

Information on a hard disk can become corrupted due to a variety of problems. If your system files are disturbed, you may find you cannot boot your system or fully utilize it. If the disk has suffered physical damage, you may or may not be able to recover your file system. If the damage is localized, you may be able to rebuild your system with a minimum of data loss. If the entire disk is damaged, you will have to replace it and recover your files from backup.

When your Unix system was installed, the disk was tested and the locations of bad tracks were recorded. Since then, additional tracks may have gone bad. If a track holding a system file goes bad, you may find that you can no longer boot from your hard disk. With an emergency-boot floppy, you may be able to recover your files. Refer to the installation document that came with your system to determine how to make an emergency-boot floppy, and keep the diskette in a safe place. *ticks HD.*

After booting from floppy disk, try to repair your hard disk with the **fsck** command. Syntax will be similar to:

```
/bin/fsck -y /dev/hd0root
```

The designation of the hard disk (here, **hd0root**) varies from one version of Unix to another.

The **fsck** command may work if your data has become scrambled, in the absence of damage to the disk. If it does not work, you must restore the root file system to your disk from backup. To do so, mount the hard-disk volume onto the boot-floppy volume. The command line is: *VIP*

```
/etc/mount /dev/hd0root /mnt
```

This command line connects the hard disk's file system with the boot floppy's file system, making the hard disk available for restoration of its files.

If you made your backup with the **backup** command, you can restore the files with the **restore** command, as follows: _tape → HD_

```
restore fr /dev/rct0 /dev/hd0root
```

This command line restores files from a raw-cartridge-tape device **rct0** to the hard-disk root file system.

If your system still fails to boot from hard disk, you probably have a serious hardware problem. If you suspect a track has gone bad, try running the **badtrk** utility in nondestructive mode. The **badtrk** utility finds faulty areas on the disk and marks them. After running it, you may be able to reinstall Unix without having to reload your other file systems.

If running **badtrk** fails to put you back in operation, your hard disk may be irreparably damaged. You may have to replace it and install your entire system again from scratch.

SUMMARY

Hard-disk backup is critical in a Unix system, as it is in any computer system. Unix offers a choice of backup media and commands. The most common backup media are floppy disks and cartridge tapes. The primary commands for hard-disk backup are **backup, cpio,** and **tar.** Each has advantages in certain situations. Make sure you understand the functions of all three before deciding which is best in a particular case.

Files that change more often should be backed up more often. It makes sense to separate files into directories based on how often they should be backed up. You can back up entire directories at once and not waste time on files that have not changed.

There is no immediate and obvious penalty for not performing a backup, but the consequences of not being backed up if the need arises can be serious. A formal backup discipline must be established and strictly followed. To make it easier, you can write a script that automatically backs up all files changed during the day. Backup tapes or diskettes should be rotated so that there are always two full backups available in addition to the one currently being created.

When you upgrade to a new version of Unix, you may need to restore some of your files from backups, relink some device drivers, and recompile some applications. The extent of the changes in the new version will determine how much you have to do.

If your disk or files become damaged, you may be able to fix the damage and recover lost information from your backups. In an extreme case, you would need to replace your hard disk, install a fresh copy of Unix on it, then restore your applications from backup.

A complete and up-to-date backup is an essential part of the solution to any lost-data problem, large or small.

## Chapter 6

Basic Unix Operations

This chapter explains how to log in and perform some basic system functions. You will see that Unix is different from DOS as soon as your system boots up. DOS assumes you are a legitimate user and, after asking for the time and date, gives you the system prompt. Unix is not so trusting. It asks you to log in before it will accept any commands. This is just the first of many differences you will encounter after stepping into the wider and more versatile world of Unix.

LOGGING IN

Before Unix will allow you to use the system, it must verify that you are an authorized user. Your name and your secret password must be on the system's list of authorized users. The system administrator, who has overall charge of the system, is responsible for adding your name and password to the list. You may then log in for the first time. The system will prompt you as follows:

```
login:
```

Respond with your assigned login name. You must spell it exactly as it was issued to you. Since Unix is case-sensitive, capitalization must also match that of the user name on file with the system.

After you have successfully entered your login name, Unix will prompt you for your secret password, as follows:

```
Password:
```

To maintain secrecy, Unix never echoes passwords to the screen as you type them (in case someone is looking over your shoulder). Particularly with systems that charge you for system time, you do not want someone else logged in under your name. Some versions of Unix, such as System V Release 3.2, will tell you when your login was last used. By comparing this login notice with the knowledge of when you actually last logged in, you can determine whether someone else logged in without your permission. If you suspect that an unauthorized person is using your login, change your password as described later in this chapter.

THE MESSAGE OF THE DAY

Once you have logged in, the system displays the message of the day, if there is one. This is a message of interest to all users and is entered by the system administrator. On a small system with only a few users, the system administrator may not bother to enter a message of the day. In that case, the next item displayed is the shell prompt.

THE SHELL PROMPT

Although you may change the shell prompt to whatever symbol you choose, each shell has a default prompt. The default prompt for the Bourne shell is the dollar sign ($). The default for the C shell is the percent sign (%).

READING THE NEWS

A feature of Unix that is absent in DOS is the **news** command. The **news** command is a communication channel from the system administrator to the system users. It accesses a repository of messages designed to keep users apprised of items of interest. You can read all current messages by issuing the **news** command without arguments:

```
$ news
```

When you read the **news**, the system notes the date and time. The next time you issue the **news** command, only messages recorded after that point will be displayed. Old messages are automatically suppressed. You can retrieve old messages by using the **-a** option with the **news** command, or you can save messages to a file as you read them.

READING YOUR MAIL

There is no provision for electronic mail under DOS, since DOS is a single-user system. Unix, however, offers two methods of exchanging mail with other users: the **mail** and **uucp** (Unix-to-Unix copy) commands. More than just a command, UUCP is an important system for exchanging files among Unix systems, usually over telephone lines via modems. The UUCP system is discussed in chapter 11.

The **mail** command is a complex, multipurpose command that sends, reads, and disposes of mail. In its simplest form (without arguments), it allows you to read any electronic-mail messages you may have received. After reading a message, you may print it, delete it, or reply to it. These options and others are also covered in chapter 11.

SENDING MAIL

The same **mail** command is used to send mail, but one or more arguments must be added. The arguments are the login IDs of the people to whom you want to send a message. For example, to send a private message to your coworker Dave, issue the command:

```
$ mail dave
```

mail send → Dave

The system will wait for you to type in your message. Only short messages should be created this way, since you can correct mistakes only on the current line. Once you have pressed [Enter], you cannot go back to that line and correct an error. When you are finished, enter [Ctrl-d] to mark the end of the message. It will be immediately routed to Dave's mailbox.

You can send a message to multiple destinations, including yourself. You may want to keep a file of all mail you have sent. One easy way is to always include yourself on the distribution list of the **mail** command. For example, if your login name is **jenny,** you might use the following command line to send a message to several of your associates:

```
$ mail val mel neil rob jim jenny
```

The message would go to five mailboxes, as well as your own.

If your message is lengthy, it may be easier to compose it with a text editor than with the **mail** command. For example, you could create a message file named **msg527.txt** with your editor and send it to the distribution list with:

```
$ mail val mel neil rob jim jenny
```

Using a text editor is explained in chapter 8.

DISPLAYING THE DATE AND TIME

DOS has a command that displays the current date and a different command that displays the current time. Unix has one command that displays both date and time. The function of the **date** command is shown in the following dialogue:

```
$ date
Sat May 27 21:46:55  PDT  1989
$
```

The system administrator can also use the **date** command to set the date to a new value.

PASSWORDS

When the system administrator assigned you a user account, both a login ID and a password came along with it. To gain access to your files, a person would need to know both. Of course, you want others to know your login ID so they can send you mail. Your password, however, should remain secret to prevent malicious or unintentional damage to your files by unauthorized users. It should be a text string that is easy for you to remember, but difficult for others to guess.

The default password assigned to you is probably easy to guess and therefore not very effective. At the first opportunity, you should change it. In fact, you should continue to change your password periodically, since someone else might discover it if they are motivated to do so. *change passwd*

To change a password, enter the **passwd** command and an argument. The argument is the login ID of the user whose password you want to change. If you enter no argument, Unix will assume that you want to change your own password. After you enter the command line, Unix will verify that you have the right to change the password by asking you to enter the old password you want to replace.

When you have correctly entered the old password, Unix prompts you for the new one. Once you have entered it, you are prompted for the new one a second time. The two entries must match before Unix will replace the password. If you make a mistake on one of the entries, you will be asked to make the entry two more times. If you succeed, the password change will be made.

The password you choose should be more than a few characters long, to make it harder to guess by trial and error. The system administrator sets the minimum password length. Usually, this is between three and eight characters.

Some systems force you to change your password periodically by *aging* it. After you have had a password for the maximum allowed interval, you must change it the next time you log in. The system administrator sets the maximum interval, which may be as few as 0 or as many as 63 weeks.

The system administrator may also specify a minimum interval, which again may be anywhere from 0 to 63 weeks. In that case, you may not change your password unless it is at least as old as the minimum interval. If you know that the secrecy of your password has been compromised and the minimum interval has not yet elapsed, you must ask the system administrator to change your password for you. The easy way around this problem is for the system administrator to always set the minimum interval to 0.

INTERRUPTING A COMMAND OR HALTING OUTPUT

You can interrupt a command that is waiting for input from the keyboard by pressing [Break] or [Del]. Thus, if you change your mind about going through with a command, in most cases you can avoid rebooting the system. This method can also be used to halt a command that is producing more output or taking longer to complete than you expected.

LOGGING OFF

When you have completed your work for the present, log off, rather than merely walk away from the system. If you are running on a system where you are charged for active time, you certainly do not want to pay for idle time. In any case, it is dangerous to leave unattended a terminal that is logged in under your ID and password. Anyone who sits down at the terminal will have access to your files and could damage them. There is no value in having a password if you leave your session open while you are away from your terminal. Form the habit of always logging off before you get up to do something else. It will take only a few seconds to log back in again.

SUMMARY

You need to know how to perform a number of basic operations in order to begin using Unix. Some of these are similar to corresponding DOS operations. Many, however, relate to the multiuser nature of Unix and have no analog in DOS.

The concept of system security, including logging in and out, passwords, and restricted access to files, is new to the person who has had experience only with single-user operating systems. New, too, is the ability to interrogate the system to see what other users are active, the facility to send and receive mail, and the ability to read news items from the system administrator.

Unix's methods of creating, navigating between, displaying, and removing directories are very similar to those of DOS. Files can be displayed and deleted in much the same way. Methods of displaying the current date and time and of halting execution of commands are also similar.

Chapter 7

Unix File Operations

The essential function of an operating system is to allow users to create files and operate on them. Different operating systems organize files differently. However, the file structure of Unix is virtually identical to that of DOS. This is no coincidence. When DOS was upgraded from Version 1 to Version 2 to support hard-disk drives, the hierarchical file structure of Unix was used as a model for the new DOS file structure.

DIRECTORIES

Both operating systems have one primary directory called the *root directory*. Within it, any number of *subdirectories* can be created. Each subdirectory can have subdirectories of its own, to as many levels as desired. Directories and subdirectories can contain both files and other subdirectories.

Creating Directories

The Unix **mkdir** command functions much like its DOS equivalent but is more general. While the DOS **mkdir** (or **md**) command creates only a single subdirectory, the Unix **mkdir** can create multiple subdirectories. For example, to create three subdirectories of the current directory and name them **temp1, temp2,** and **temp3,** issue the command:

```
$ mkdir temp1 temp2 temp3
```

To accomplish the same thing with DOS, you would need to issue three separate **mkdir** (or **md**) commands.

Another difference is that DOS allows anyone to create a subdirectory anywhere. Unix allows a user to create a subdirectory of a "parent" directory only if the user has *write* permission for that parent. (See chapter 9 for an explanation of access permissions.) This feature protects a user's directory from becoming cluttered with unauthorized subdirectories.

Changing Directories

The Unix **cd** command is similar to, but not identical to, the DOS **cd** (or **chdir**) command. When used with a directory name as an argument, **cd**, in both DOS and Unix, makes the directory named in the argument the current one. When the **cd** command is used with no argument, however, the actions under Unix and DOS differ. Under DOS, the terminal always displays the name of the current directory. Under Unix, the situation is more complicated.

Every user in a Unix system is assigned a home directory to which he or she is automatically routed after logging in. From there, the **cd** command can be used with the appropriate argument to move to a different directory. When a **cd** command is issued without an argument, execution is transferred to the home directory, because the home directory is the default argument of the Unix **cd** command.

Removing Directories

The Unix rmdir and the DOS **rmdir** (or **rd**) commands are related to each other in much the same way that the **mkdir** commands are. Under both operating systems, **rmdir** removes the directory specified in the argument only if the directory is empty. But Unix is more flexible; it allows you to remove multiple empty directories by specifying multiple arguments, while the DOS **rmdir** (or **rd**) command can remove only one directory. Thus, the following Unix command removes all three directories (**temp1, temp2,** and **temp3**) in a single operation:

```
$ rmdir temp1 temp2 temp3
```

Dos. (\)
Unix (/).

CD .. — parent dir
cd .. — current dir

PATHS

The concept of *paths* between directories is the same in Unix and DOS. A superficial difference is that a DOS directory is separated from its subdirectories by backslashes (\), while a Unix directory is separated from its subdirectories by forward slashes (/). In both operating systems, the current directory is denoted by a dot (.) and the current directory's parent by a double dot (..).

In the example shown in figure 7-1, the home directory is named **allen** and has two subdirectories, **letters** and **memos**. You can move among them with the **cd** command.

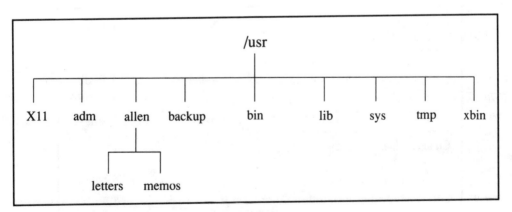

Figure 7-1. The allen tree directory

from Letters → allen
 # cd ..
to use
 # ../..

from Letters → Memos
 # cd ../memos.

61

If you are in **letters** and want to move to **allen,** use the following command:

```
$ cd ..
```

To move from **letters** to **memos,** use the following command:

```
$ cd ../memos
```

It is even possible to move directly from the current directory to a "grandparent" directory with the following command:

```
$ cd ../..
```

DETERMINING WHERE YOU ARE

Under DOS, you can always determine what directory you are in by issuing a **cd** command without an argument. Under Unix, the sole function of the **cd** command is to change directories. A different command, **pwd,** identifies the current directory. The only purpose of the **pwd** command is to print the path name of the current working directory.

Table 7-1 summarizes the Unix and DOS commands that deal with directories.

Table 7-1. Functions of Unix and DOS directory commands

FUNCTION	UNIX	DOS
Create a new directory	mkdir dir1	mkdir dir1
Create two new directories	mkdir dir1 dir2	mkdir dir1 mkdir dir2
Change to **letters** directory	cd /letters	cd \letters
Change to parent directory	cd ..	cd ..
Change to home directory	cd	N/A
Print working directory path	pwd	cd
Remove an existing directory	rmdir dir1	rmdir dir1
Remove two existing directories	rmdir dir1 dir2	rmdir dir1 rmdir dir2

SYSTEM DIRECTORIES

When you install a DOS system on your hard disk, only one directory is created, the root directory. Most people copy the DOS utilities into the root directory and promptly forget about them. New subdirectories are created as needed to accommodate the user's application files.

Unix is a much more extensive and complex operating system than DOS. When you install a Unix system, a number of subdirectories are automatically created and are filled with different kinds of system files. Figure 7-2 shows a typical newly installed file system with system directories.

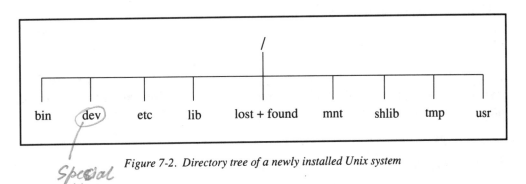

Special
files

Figure 7-2. Directory tree of a newly installed Unix system

Each subdirectory contains a collection of related files. There are three types of files: ordinary, directory, and special.

Ordinary Files

Ordinary files, which include program files and data files, are the kind you generally think of when you hear the word *file*. A file is the basic structure an operating system uses to store information. Such files can be read from and written to; program files can also be executed. There is no fundamental difference between a file in a Unix system and one in a DOS system. Although their file formats are not compatible with each other, they serve the same purposes.

Directory Files

In both DOS and Unix, subdirectories are actually no more than files. Each directory file contains information about the files "contained" in that directory. The Unix directory file contains a little more information than its DOS counterpart. For example, a Unix directory includes the access rights of various groups of users. In basic function, however, directory files in the two operating systems are the same.

Special (Device) Files

peripheral devices are treated like files (device files)

In both Unix and DOS, peripheral devices such as terminals, printers, disk drives, tape drives, and communications lines are treated like files. Under Unix, they are called *special files*, or *device files*, and file-management commands operate on them just as if they were true disk files. By convention, these device files are contained in the **/dev** directory.

The **cp** command illustrates the identical treatment Unix gives to both ordinary files and device files. For example, you may want to copy a text file and give it a different name in the current directory. The command to use is:

```
cp textfile newfile
```

The DOS **copy** command is used in a similar way.

printer — send file to printer

You can also copy from a device to a file and vice versa. For example, the following Unix command puts the text file out on the line printer:

```
cp textfile /dev/lp0
```
cp boris_file /dev/pr.

In DOS, copying from a device to a file and from a file to a device is handled in a similar manner.

The following Unix command line shows how you can display a text file to your terminal screen:

```
cp textfile /dev/tty01
```
cp boris_file /dev/tty01   Display on the screen

This example assumes that the terminal is identified as **tty01**. (Unix generally uses the **tty** designation for terminal devices.)

CREATING FILES DIRECTLY FROM THE KEYBOARD

The familiar DOS technique for creating a short text file directly from the keyboard also works with Unix. A DOS example would be:

```
copy con test.bat/a
cd /games
dir
^z
```

The preceding example creates a batch file that causes the directory **games** to become the current directory and the files in that directory to be listed on the terminal screen. [Ctrl-z] is the DOS end-of-file character.

An equivalent Unix example is:

```
cp /dev/tty01 test
cd /usr/games
ls -l
^d
```

When executed, this short Unix program changes the current directory to **/usr/games** and displays a list of its files. Under Unix, [Ctrl-d] is the end-of-file character.

RESTRICTING ACCESS TO YOUR FILES

When you create a file, you are considered to be its owner. Since Unix is a multiuser system, you may want to restrict access to your files. Perhaps not everyone with access to the system should have access to your files. Similarly, you may not be authorized to use files created by another user. Restricting access to your files is addressed in detail in chapter 9.

NAMING FILES

The file-naming conventions for Unix are similar to those used by DOS, though Unix is somewhat more flexible. Any legal DOS file name would also be legal under Unix. Some Unix file names, however, would not be legal under DOS.

A DOS file name consists of three parts. The first part is mandatory and consists of a name from one to eight characters in length. The second part is a dot (.), which is needed only if the optional third part is present. Dots may not appear anywhere else in the file name. The third part is called an *extension*, which, if used, may be from one to three characters in length.

The form of a file name in Unix is less restrictive than that of a DOS file name. Unix file names may be from one to fourteen characters in length and may contain multiple periods (.). There is no distinction between names and extensions.

[handwritten margin note: Unix may have extension may or may not]

USING METACHARACTERS (WILDCARDS)

Both DOS and Unix allow you to use *metacharacters*, commonly called *wildcards*, to operate with a single command on multiple files. DOS has two wildcard characters: the asterisk (*) and the question mark (?). Unix has three: the asterisk, the question mark, and square brackets ([ ]).

The function of the asterisk is similar in both Unix and DOS. It matches any string of characters, including the null string. Thus, the following command will list the name of every file in the current directory:

```
ls *
```

The following command will list every file that starts with the letters *repo:*

```
ls repo*
```

Note that files named **report1, report2, report10,** and **repossessions** would be listed, but **reprint** would not.

There are minor differences in the function of the asterisk in the two operating systems. In Unix, the following command lists all files in the current directory:

```
ls *
```

If one of the files is a directory, its name will end in a colon (:), and all the files in it will be listed also.

The equivalent DOS command lists all files in the current directory, but directory files are not distinguished in any way:

```
dir *.*
```

The question-mark (?) wildcard works the same in both operating systems. It matches any single character. Thus, the following command would retrieve the files **report1** and **report2**, but not **report10:**

```
ls report?
```

The brackets ([ ]) wildcard lets you specify a *set* of characters. It is considered a match if a file name contains any one character in the specified place. Of the files **report1, report2,** and **reports,** the following command would retrieve **report1** and **report2,** but not **reports:**

```
ls report[1234567]
```

Brackets can also be used with a *range of values*. The preceding command could have been written as follows to achieve the same result:

```
ls report[1-7]
```

very good!

Similarly, you can also specify a *range of letters*. Remember that, in Unix, uppercase letters are distinguished from lowercase.

DISPLAYING A LIST OF FILES

The Unix equivalent of the DOS **dir** command is the **ls** command (short for "list"). The **ls** command, like many Unix commands, accepts various options and arguments that affect the output display. The options are described in detail in the user reference guide that came with your Unix system. Table 7-2 shows some common uses of the **ls** command and the corresponding DOS **dir** command.

*Table 7-2. The Unix **ls** command and the DOS **dir** command*

FUNCTION	UNIX	DOS
List filenames in multiple columns	ls	dir /w
List filenames with file attributes	ls -l	dir
List attributes for a single file	ls filename.ext	dir filename.ext
List all files that start with "file"	ls file*	dir file*.*

DISPLAYING FILES

Some files are understandable to humans and some are understandable only to computers. For Unix and DOS, the former are those in which the information is stored in ASCII (American Standard Code for Information Interchange). The code is translated into letters, numbers, and symbols before being displayed on the screen. ASCII files, sometimes called *text files* or *source files,* are the only ones it is worthwhile to display.

The cat Command

In Unix, the most common way to display an ASCII file on the terminal screen is with the **cat** command. The **cat** command was designed to concatenate, or join, multiple files, displaying them in the process. However, its most common use is to display the contents of a single file. When used with a single file name as an argument, **cat** works just like the DOS **type** command. The following command displays the contents of **file.txt** on the screen:

```
cat file.txt
```

If you are using **cat** only to display a file, you should use the default option of sending the output to the terminal screen for display. However, if you are using **cat** to create a file made up of several smaller files, you should redirect output from the screen to a file on disk. For more information, see "Combining Files" later in this chapter.

The most commonly used DOS command for displaying the contents of a file on the terminal screen is the **type** command. The following DOS command displays the contents of the specified file:

```
type filename
```

In DOS, there are other ways to display the contents of a file. For instance, the following command will copy the file to the console, which has the effect of displaying it on the console screen. The display is the same as that produced by the **type** command:

```
copy filename con
```

The more Command

The Unix **more** command is a filter. It provides a second way of displaying the contents of an ASCII file. The primary job of the **more** command is to display the contents of a text file, pausing the display each time the screen fills. Pressing the space bar displays the next screenful. If the file is shorter than one screenful, the **more** command acts just like **cat**: the file is displayed, then control is returned to the shell.

The Unix **more** command supports a large number of options. You can specify the number of lines you want to display, from one to the maximum number supported by your terminal. There are other options helpful in specific situations.

DOS also has a **more** command, but it is much more restricted. The DOS **more** filter cannot be executed from the shell prompt; it must receive its input either from a pipe (pipes are discussed in chapter 12) or from a redirected input. After the DOS **more** command pauses the display, pressing any key will display the next screenful. There are no other options.

The pg Command

Like the **more** filter, the Unix **pg** command is a filter that allows you to peruse a text file one page at a time. Again, you can specify the size of the page. The **pg** command, however, allows you to scroll the display backward as well as forward. Another option available with **pg** is searching a file for a specified set of characters. This search can also be performed both forward and backward.

DOS does not let you scroll backward through a file, but its **find** filter does search a file for a specified pattern. Thus, the Unix **pg** filter combines some of the capabilities of the DOS **type, more,** and **find** filters. In addition, the **pg** filter does things that no combination of DOS commands can do.

The pr Command

The **pr** command prints the contents of text files on the standard output device. It differs from the **cat, more,** and **pg** filters in giving you considerable control over the format of the output. You can control vertical and horizontal spacing and offsets, and you can even display output in a multicolumn format. See chapter 15 for more information on printing files.

File Display Summary

Table 7-3 compares the Unix text-display commands with related DOS commands.

Table 7-3. Unix and DOS text-file display commands

FUNCTION	UNIX	DOS
Display an ASCII file on the terminal screen	cat filename	type filename
Display an ASCII file one screenful at a time	more filename	more < filename or filename | more
Find the first occurrence of a specified text string and display it along with the following screenful of data	pg + /pattern/filename	N/A
Display contents of a text file in two columns	pr -2 filename	N/A

MOVING FILES BETWEEN DIRECTORIES

With hierarchical directory systems such as those of DOS and Unix, you may sometimes want to move a file from one subdirectory to another. Under DOS, this is usually a two-step process. First, the file is copied from its current location to the new location. Second, the old copy is deleted. Unix can accomplish the same result in a single step.

The mv Command

The Unix **mv** command moves one or more files from one directory to another in a single operation. After execution, the specified files are present in the new directory and absent from the original directory. To move two files from the current directory to one named **/usr/allison,** use the following syntax:

```
$ mv file1 file2 /usr/allison
```

The cp Command

You can also move Unix files in a two-step process similar to that in DOS. First, use the **cp** command to copy an existing file into a different directory. Then use the **rm** command to remove the original copy of the file. Typical syntax would be:

```
$ cp filename /usr/allison
$ rm filename
```

The copy Command

The Unix **copy** command can be used to copy some or all of the files in one directory to another. For example, to copy all the files starting with the letter x from the current directory to one named **/usr/tmp,** issue the command:

```
$ copy x* /usr/tmp
```

The **copy** command can also be used to copy a single file from one directory to another. When used for this purpose, it acts exactly like the **cp** command.

RENAMING FILES

Using the DOS **rename** command, giving a file a new name and/or location is a straightforward operation. Unix's **mv** command can be used to rename a file as well as move one. The renamed file can be in the original file's directory or in another one. Thus, the DOS command **rename file file2** has the same effect as the Unix command **mv file file2.**

COMBINING FILES

As mentioned earlier in this chapter, one function of the Unix **cat** command is to concatenate files. The DOS **copy** command also provides for the concatenation of files. For example, under DOS you could combine three text files containing essays into a single collection of essays as follows:

```
C:>copy essay1.txt + essay2.txt + essay3.txt collect.txt
```

You could add additional essays to the collection by appending them to the collection file. The syntax would be:

```
C:>copy collect.txt + essay4.txt + essay5.txt
```

Since no destination argument is specified, the first source argument is assumed to be the destination of the other source files. The file **collect.txt** now contains the text of all five essays.

Under Unix, the **cat** command achieves the same result, but with somewhat different syntax. To specify where to send the concatenated essay files, you must use redirection of output. To create the essay collection, use the command:

```
$ cat essay1 essay2 essay3 > collection
```

Note that since Unix allows longer file names, they can be more descriptive.

To add additional essays to the collection, use the append operator:

```
$ cat essay4 essay5 >> collection
```

The resulting collection of essays will be exactly the same as the collection created in the preceding DOS example using **copy.**

DELETING FILES

To delete files that are no longer needed, DOS uses the **erase** command, also known as **del.** Syntax is simple:

```
C:>del filename
```

A wildcard file name can be used to delete a group of files with one command.

DOS allows only one directory entry for each file, but Unix allows several. You may have any number of entries (or links) in any number of directories, all referring to the same file. The advantage is that multiple users can access a file from their own directories without having to duplicate it. Not only does this save disk space, it prevents the creation of differing versions of the same file.

The Unix **rm** command removes only the entry in the current directory, not the file itself. The file itself is removed only if the entry being removed is the last entry on the disk. The **rm** command with the **-r** argument can also be used to remove a directory, including all the files and subdirectories it contains. This feature can save time, but can also be dangerous. Be sure you know what is in the target directory's subdirectories, since they will be deleted whether you look at them or not.

Multiple unrelated files can be removed with a single **rm** command. A typical **rm** command might be:

```
$ rm file1 file2 file3
```

The Unix **rmdir** command, which removes an empty directory, is similar to the DOS **rmdir** command. However, the Unix command removes only an entry for a directory, while the DOS command removes the directory itself. If there is only one entry remaining for the directory specified by a Unix **rmdir** command, the directory is removed. Thus, the Unix **rmdir** command has the same effect as the DOS **rmdir** command if there is only one copy of the directory left to be removed.

Table 7-4 compares the DOS and Unix commands for moving, renaming, combining, and deleting files.

Table 7-4. Unix and DOS commands for moving, renaming, concatenating, and deleting files

FUNCTION	UNIX	DOS
Move a file from current directory to another directory named /usr/tmp	mv file1 /usr/tmp	copy file1 /usr/tmp del file1
Move two unrelated files from the current directory to a directory named /usr/tmp	mv file1 file2 /usr/tmp	copy file1 /usr/tmp copy file2 /usr/tmp del file1 del file2
Rename a file without moving it to another directory	mv file1 file2	rename file1 file2
Move a file to another directory, renaming it in the process	mv file1 /usr/tmp/ file2	copy file1 /usr/tmp/file2
Combine two files, creating a third	cat file1 file2 > file3	copy file1+file2 file3
Append a file to an existing file	cat file4 >> file3	copy file3+file4
Remove a file from the current directory	rm filename	erase filename or del filename
Remove two files from the current directory	rm file2 file2	del file1 del file2

STANDARD INPUT AND STANDARD OUTPUT

Although there are other ways of communicating with the Unix system, the two most common are called *standard input* and *standard output*. Standard input directs a stream of characters from a designated input device to the currently running program. Standard output directs the stream of output characters from the currently running program to a designated output device.

default.

The default input device is the terminal keyboard, and the default output device is the terminal screen. You may sometimes want to take input from another source or send output to another destination. This is accomplished with a process called *redirection*, described later in this chapter.

The use of standard input and standard output is important because it gives Unix much of its flexibility. Unix commands and programs assume that data arrive and leave in an unformatted character stream. Because of this common data interface, commands can be combined in any manner desired without concern for whether such combinations will work. You can be sure that any legal sequence of commands will produce the correct result, even if you have never used it before.

STANDARD ERROR

In addition to the two primary input/output (I/O) streams, standard input and standard output, there is a third stream called *standard error.* When the system detects an error, such as an illegal command entered at the keyboard, it puts an error message out on the standard-error channel.

The default standard-error device is the terminal screen, so normally you will see standard-error messages mixed in with standard-output messages on the screen. You can separate the two streams by redirecting one or both to a different file or output device.

REDIRECTION

Although standard output normally goes to the terminal screen, it can be sent to a different output device or to a file through the use of a redirection operator. The output redirection operator is the "greater-than" sign (>).

The **ls** command sends a list of files in a directory to the standard output. Using the output redirection operator, you can direct the list to a file or to an alternate output device, such as a printer. Once the list is stored in a file, you can use additional commands to extract useful information from it. A sample output-redirection command is:

```
$ ls > listfile
```

Input redirection is the complementary operation. The input redirection operator (<) specifies a file or alternate input device (other than the default keyboard) from which to take input. In Unix, the command is always the first item on a command line, so the input or output redirection is specified after the command. For example, the following command line takes the text stored in **sourcefile** as input. It then sends the received text to the standard output, which in this case is redirected to a file named **destfile:**

```
$ cat < sourcefile > destfile
```

Standard error, sometimes called diagnostic output, has a redirection symbol of its own, the "two-greater-than" sign (2>). You may want to redirect ordinary output to one file and error messages to another, or you may want to view ordinary output on the screen, saving any error messages in a file for later perusal. The following command line illustrates the syntax for this situation:

```
$ mv filename /usr/allen 2> errorfile
```

Many users keep a file, or log, of error messages, recording any errors that occur when commands are being executed. Every time an error occurs, the associated error message is appended to the log. To append an error message to an existing file, rather than replace a previous message, use the "two-double-greater-than" standard error operator (2>>). The following example illustrates the syntax:

```
$ mv v86.h /usr/allen 2>> /usr/allen/errorlog
```

When the command is executed, messages such as the following will be sent to the **errorlog** file and appended to any messages that may already be stored there:

```
mv: cannot unlink v86.h
mv: Permission denied
```

The "double-greater-than" sign (>>) can be used for appending new information to standard output in the same way that the "two-double-greater-than" sign (2>>) is used to append new information to standard error.

FILTERS

Filters are programs that take standard input, modify it in some way, then send it to standard output. The **more** and **pg** commands discussed earlier are examples of filters. They take a text stream, insert some code that modifies how the text will be displayed, then send the result to standard output. Unix has quite a large number of filters; DOS has only three: **sort, find,** and **more.**

Filters are particularly useful when strung together and executed sequentially. This process of executing a sequence of commands is called *piping*.

PIPES

A pipe is a logical structure that takes the output of one command and directs it to the input of another command. A sequence of commands joined in this way is called a *pipeline*. The pipe operator is the vertical bar (|). The *output* of the command to the left of the operator is the *input* for the command to the right. For example, suppose you have an unsorted list of client names in a last name-first name format in a file named **client.unsort.** You want to display the list in sorted order on your terminal screen, and you want the display to pause after each scrreenful of names. To accomplish this, you would use the following command line:

```
$ cat client.unsort | sort | more
```

In the above example, the **cat** command sends the unsorted client list to standard output. The first pipe in the pipeline sends the list to the **sort** filter, which alphabetizes the list. The output of the **sort** filter is then piped to the input of the **more** filter. The **more** filter pauses the display after each full screen of names.

COMPOUND COMMANDS

The preceding example also provided an illustration of a *compound command:* in this case, the **cat** command followed by two filters. Redirection of standard input, standard output, and standard error can also appear in a command pipeline. All these operators may be used together to produce a desired result. For example, the following command line concatenates the unsorted file named **newclient. uns** with the existing unsorted client file and pipes the resulting combined file to the **sort** filter. The **sort** filter in turn sends the sorted result to the file **client.sort.** If the **cat** command were to fail for any reason, the error message would be appended to the **errorlog** file:

```
$ cat newclient.uns >> client.unsort 2>> errorlog | sort > client.sort
```

BACKGROUND PROCESSING

Unlike DOS, Unix is a multitasking operating system; two or more tasks or processes can run at the same time. It would be confusing if several active processes were all requesting input from the keyboard or sending output to the terminal screen at the same time. To prevent confusion, the system distinguishes between *foreground* and *background* processes.

The foreground process is the one that communicates with the terminal. Each user can have only one foreground process active at any given time. Background processes do not have access to the terminal. Any number of background processes may be operating at once. Normally, you would use input and output redirection with background processes. While a background process cannot communicate with the terminal, it can accept input that has been redirected from a file. It can also redirect its output to another file.

Background processing allows you to get much more work done than would be possible if you had to wait for each job to finish running before starting another. Lengthy jobs not requiring interaction with the user are good candidates for background processing. After you launch a background process, the shell prompt returns immediately, allowing you to work on other tasks while the background job is executing. The system will not notify the user of completion. To see if the background process is still executing, issue the **ps** command, which displays the status of all active processes. If your background process is still active, its process ID will be listed. If not, the process ID will not be listed.

The background-process operator is the ampersand (**&**). To execute a command in the background, type the command and add an ampersand as the last character on the command line. The system will display the process ID number that it has assigned to the background process, then immediately display the shell prompt. You may now enter other commands. The background process has been launched and is executing. If you have redirected all terminal I/O to the background process, there will be no further indication of its progress on the screen.

If you intend to run a process in the background, you should redirect its input and output to keep them from interfering with the foreground process. A background process cannot expect any input from the keyboard. Redirect input to a file that contains the needed keystrokes. Similarly, output should be redirected to a file, so the output is not displayed on the screen. It could be mixed with the screen output of the foreground job, creating a confusing display. You can inspect the contents of the output file later to see if the background job executed correctly.

An example of how to launch a background process is given in the following example:

```
$ cat file1 file2 file3 > bigfile | sort > sortfile &
311
$
```

In the example, 311 is the process ID assigned to the background process. The shell prompt is displayed on the next line; the system is ready for your next command.

SUMMARY

The structure of the Unix file system is very similar to that of DOS. Both have a hierarchical file structure, and many of the commands used to create, manipulate, and delete files in Unix are similar to their DOS counterparts. Unix files are contained in directories related to one another in a tree-like structure. You can navigate from one directory to another by specifying the path that connects them.

Directories contain ordinary files, and directories are themselves files. Many of the commands designed to manipulate ordinary files will also work on directory files. Peripheral devices, such as terminals, printers, and disk drives, are also treated by Unix as if they were files. Thus, one file-manipulation command can be used in several ways, depending on whether it is used with an ordinary file, a directory file, or a device file.

The structure of a Unix file is somewhat more complex than that of a DOS file, because Unix is a multiuser environment. There must be a mechanism for determining who has the right to read, modify, and execute each file. The Unix permissions system allows file owners to decide what access permissions to give themselves, to other users in their group, and to all others on the system.

Unix files are accessed by their names. File names may include any valid ASCII characters and may be up to 14 characters in length. Wildcard characters can be used to specify ambiguous file names, thus operating on multiple files with a single command.

Several commands are available for displaying the contents of a file, and several more for transferring a file from one directory to another. Other commands rename and delete files. Redirection, pipes, and filters give the user considerable flexibility in performing complex tasks with a single command line.

Finally, individual users can take advantage of the multitasking ability of Unix by running background processes simultaneously with a foreground task with which they are interacting. Multitasking dramatically increases the efficiency of a Unix system.

Chapter **8**

Basic Text Processing

Text files are generated and modified with a text editor. Nearly all implementations of Unix include at least two text editors: **ed** and **vi.** The first, **ed**, is a *line editor.* Line editors were designed to be used with old-fashioned printing terminals such as mechanical Teletype machines and DECwriters. All activity takes place on the current line, since such terminals cannot back up to a previous line.

The second text editor generally included with Unix is **vi,** a *screen editor.* Screen editors were designed for use with video terminals. With **vi,** a user has full cursor control, meaning modifications can be made anywhere on the screen and in any desired order. Today, video terminals are universally used, so this chapter will cover the use of the **vi** editor. Once you have mastered **vi,** you may never need **ed.**

CREATING A FILE

To create a new file using the vi screen editor, simply specify the file name. For example, the following command line will clear the screen, put the cursor in the upper-left corner, and display a column of tildes (~) down the left side of the screen. Each tilde marks a blank line, on which new text may be entered:

```
$ vi newfile
```

With **vi**, there are two main operational modes: *command* and *text entry*. When you enter **vi**, you are automatically in command mode. In command mode, you can move the cursor around, alter existing text, and search existing text; however, you cannot add text. Text entry mode lets you add text either by appending or by inserting. Appending adds text starting at the position immediately to the right of the cursor. Inserting adds text at the current cursor position.

TEXT ENTRY

To append text to a file, place the cursor just to the left of the character where you want to enter new text and press the [a] key. The cursor will move one space to the right. Any text you type now will be added to your file at the point where you placed the cursor. You can proceed from one line to the next either by pressing [Return] whenever you want to end a line or by letting the text wrap to the next line by itself.

To insert text in an existing file or to start entering text in a new file, place the cursor at the point where you want to enter new text. Then press the [i] key and begin typing text.

To leave a text entry mode, press [Esc]. This returns you to command mode.

SHOWING THE OPERATIONAL MODE

At a given moment, you may not always know which mode you are in, since there is no mode indication on the screen. You can put such an indication on the screen if you wish by using one of the last-line commands. The mode indications resulting from a last-line command are displayed, as the name suggests, on the last line of the screen. Last-line commands always start with a colon (:).

The command **:set showmode** will display the current operational mode in the lower-right corner of the screen, except for command mode. In the **vi** editor, you can always get to command mode by pressing [Esc]. If you happen to be in command mode and press [Esc], the computer may flash or beep.

MOVING THE CURSOR

Most keyboards have cursor-control keys marked with up, down, left, and right arrows. These keys provide a convenient means for moving the cursor around on the screen when you are in command mode. If your keyboard does not have these keys, or if you are in a text entry mode, you can use the following keys instead:

h	moves the cursor left one character
j	moves the cursor down one line
k	moves the cursor up one line
l	moves the cursor right one character

In addition, pressing [spacebar] moves the cursor one character to the right and pressing [backspace] moves it one character to the left. If you precede any cursor-movement key with an integer (2, 3, 4, etc.), the cursor will move the specified number of characters or lines; otherwise it moves only one character or line. If there are not enough characters or lines in the direction you specify, the terminal will beep to tell you that the editor cannot comply with your instruction.

DELETING TEXT

There are several commands for deleting text. The **x** command will delete the character at the cursor position. The *n*x command will delete a number (*n*) of characters, starting from the cursor position. The **dw** command deletes the current word; *n*dw deletes *n* words starting with the current word. The **dd** command deletes the current line; *n*dd deletes *n* lines starting at the current line. The **d{** and **d}** commands delete the rest of the current paragraph, starting from the cursor position.

SEARCHING FOR A STRING

Usually, the quickest way to find a particular point in a text file is to search for a character string. The **/string** command searches forward from the current cursor position for the first occurrence of the string, and the **?string** command searches backward. Both commands place the cursor at the first character of the specified string. The **n** command repeats the last string search command, and the **N** command reverses the direction of the search. Thus, if you are searching backward through the file for a particular occurrence of the specified string, the **?string** command will find the first one prior to your starting cursor position. Pressing **n** will move the cursor to the next previous occurrence of the string. You can proceed in this fashion until you find the instance you are looking for. At any point, you can press **N** to start searching in the opposite direction (in this case, forward).

OPENING A NEW LINE

You may want to insert one or more blank lines between two existing lines of text. There are two commands for this operation. The **o** command inserts a blank line just below the line where the cursor is currently located; the **O** command inserts a blank line just above.

MODIFYING TEXT

You can modify text in two steps: first deleting existing text and then appending new text in its place. It is also possible to modify text in a single operation. Unix offers three such methods: replacing, substituting, and changing.

Replacing Text

Three commands are available for replacing text, although none is very handy. The simplest, **r**, replaces a single character with a new one. Move the cursor to the character you want to change, press **r**, then type the new character. You remain in command mode while using this replacement technique. The usefulness of this command is limited because only one character can be replaced.

The *nrc* command is even less useful. The *n* specifies the number of characters to be replaced. The *c* specifies what the replacement character will be. Starting at the cursor position and moving right, this command will replace *n* characters of existing text with *n* repetitions of the character *c*. Consider the following line of text:

```
The replace command is superfluous.
```

Place the cursor on the first letter *s* in the word *superfluous,* then issue the following command:

```
11rx
```

The result is:

```
The replace command is xxxxxxxxxxx.
```

This is a good way to censor objectionable material, but does not seem to have much value otherwise.

The **R** command is only somewhat more useful. It replaces multiple characters starting at the current cursor position and moving right. However, the number of characters you enter must exactly match the number of characters being replaced. After entering the desired number of characters, press [Esc] to return to command mode.

Substituting Text

The commands for substituting text are analogous to those for replacing text, but are more flexible. The **s** command deletes the character at the cursor position, then allows you to append as many characters as you want. You must press [Esc] when you are finished to return to command mode. The *n***s** command deletes *n* characters starting at the cursor position and moving right, then appends characters until you press [Esc]. The **S** command replaces all the characters on the current line with the new text that you enter.

Changing Text

The commands for changing text are the most useful. They operate on text objects such as words, sentences, and paragraphs, as opposed to characters. The change command deletes all characters from the current cursor position to the end of the current word (**cw**), sentence (**c)**), or paragraph (**c}**), and replaces them with the text you enter immediately following the command.

CUTTING AND PASTING

The **vi** editor allows you to move a section of text to another location in the file. This is a two-step operation. The block of text is first removed (cut) from its current location, then inserted (pasted) in a new location.

The first part of a cut-and-paste operation, the cut, may be performed with the delete commands explained in the preceding paragraphs. To prevent irrecoverable data loss, **vi** always keeps the most recent deletion in a temporary buffer. If you change your mind about a deletion, you can recover the deleted text from the buffer by executing the **p** (put) command.

The temporary buffer feature and the **p** command can also be used to move text within a file. Simply delete the text, move the cursor to the desired location, and issue the **p** command. The text will be retrieved from the buffer and inserted in its new location.

Remember that the temporary buffer holds only the *latest* deleted text or copied text. Should you delete another passage before pasting the first one, the first passage is overwritten in the buffer.

An alternate method of performing the cut-and-paste operation uses the **y** (yank) command. The **y** command *copies* a specified text object into a temporary yank buffer just like the one that holds the most recent deletion. However, the text that is placed in the yank buffer is not deleted from the main body of text; it is only *copied*. Thus, the yank method of performing a cut-and-paste is safer than the delete method. The text you want to move is less likely to be overwritten by an interposed operation.

When you yank a text object (word, sentence, or paragraph) from your file, it is not removed from its original location. If you want to replicate a text object one or more times, a yank followed by a series of pastes will do the job. But if you want only to move the text object once, you must go back and delete it in its original location after you have yanked and pasted it to its new location. (In this case the delete command is more efficient.)

It is possible to move several text blocks simultaneously by using registers. There are 26 registers, each identified by a letter. You can either delete or yank a different text object into each one, then paste the objects into new locations as necessary. Consider the following example:

```
This is sentence one. This is sentence two. This is sentence three.
```

Place the cursor at the first character of the first sentence, then issue the following command:

```
3"ay)
```

This command says, "Yank three sentences starting from the current cursor position and place them into register *a*." Now place the cursor two spaces after the end of the third sentence and issue the following command:

```
"ap
```

This command says, "Take the contents of register a and put it at the current cursor position." The result is as follows:

```
This is sentence one. This is sentence two. This is sentence three.
This is sentence one. This is sentence two. This is sentence three.
```

If you had wanted to move the three sentences rather than replicate them, you would have substituted the delete command for the yank command.

QUITTING

After an editing session, you must decide whether to save the changes you have made to your file. So far, these changes have been made in a buffer. Nothing has been written out to disk yet. If you decide you want to save your work, press **ZZ**. The buffer will be saved to the file you named when you first called **vi**, and you will be returned to the shell prompt.

If you decide not to save your work, press **:q**. When you issue the **:q** command, **vi** protects you from inadvertently destroying your work, by displaying a message such as the following:

```
No write since last change (:quit! overrides)
```

This gives you a chance to reconsider whether you want to save your work. If you indeed want to quit without saving, append the *bang* sign (!) to the quit command, as illustrated in the following:

```
:q!
```

SUMMARY OF COMMON COMMANDS

Table 8-1 lists some commonly used **vi** commands and briefly describes their functions. For more information on these and other **vi** commands, refer to the user reference guide for your implementation of Unix.

*Table 8-1. Common **vi** editing commands*

Text Entry Mode

a	Enter text after current cursor position
i	Enter text at current cursor position
A	Enter text at end of current line
I	Enter text at beginning of current line
o	Open a blank line below current cursor position
O	Open a blank line above current cursor position
[Backspace]	Delete character to left of cursor
[Esc]	Return to command mode

Cursor Movement

h	Move cursor one space to left
j	Move cursor one line down
k	Move cursor one line up
l	Move cursor one space toright
[Space]	Move cursor one space to right
[Backspace]	Move cursor one space to left
e	Move cursor to end of current word
w	Move cursor to beginning of next word
$	Move cursor to end of current line
^	Move cursor to beginning of current line

Text Deletion

x	Delete character at cursor
dw	Delete word at cursor
dd	Delete current line
D	Delete from cursor to end of line

Table 8-1 (continued)

Text Modification

r	Replace character at cursor
s	Delete character at cursor and append text
cw	Replace word with new text
c)	Replace sentence with new text
c}	Replace paragraph with new text
cc	Replace current line with new text
C	Replace from cursor position to end of line with new text

Miscellaneous Functions

u	Undo last command
/	Search forward for a text string
?	Search backward for a text string
n	Go to next occurrence of search string
.	Repeat previous action
y	Yank a copy of a text object
yw	Yank a copy of a word
y	Yank a copy of current line
y)	Yank text up to end of current sentence
y}	Yank text up to end of current paragraph
"*xyn*	Put a copy of text-object *n* into register *x*
p	Put yanked text at position to right of cursor
P	Put yanked text at cursor position
ZZ	Write to file and quit **vi**
[Esc]	Cancel previous command

Last-line Mode

:w	Write to file
:q	Quit
:wq	Write to file, then quit
:set	Change options
:!	Escape shell

SUMMARY

The Unix screen editor **vi** contains all the tools needed to create and edit text files. Commands for adding text, moving around within existing text, and deleting text, are supplemented by commands that allow you to search for a pattern, modify existing text, and move blocks of text from one location to another within a file. The large number of **vi** commands provides great flexibility in text manipulation.

Chapter 9

Multiuser Operation

T he ability to support multiple users at multiple terminals is built into the basic structure of Unix. The operations of one active user can affect the operations of another. Therefore, Unix contains safeguards to prevent unwanted interaction between simultaneously executing tasks. It also provides the mechanisms to facilitate communication between tasks when interaction is desired.

This chapter deals with the safeguards that protect a user from outside interference. The next chapter explains how separate tasks can be made to work cooperatively.

THE UNIX SECURITY SYSTEM

The Unix security system is layered; if an unauthorized user breaches one layer, there are additional hurdles to overcome before sensitive data can be accessed.

The first layer of security is the login operation itself. As explained in chapter 3, to gain access to the system, a user must enter a valid user name and secret password. The login name is echoed on the screen as it is entered. The password, however, is not echoed; therefore, even very observant bystanders are prevented from learning the password. A user who has successfully logged in will still find that access to files is controlled only by the file's owner, who specifies write and execute permissions.

The necessity of logging in with a secret password, the division of users into three categories (file owner, group, and anyone else), and the file-access permission structure all work together to ensure the security of the information stored on the system.

The Login Structure

Before you can use a Unix system, you must identify yourself by logging in. The system maintains a list of authorized users and will grant access only to people on that list. Chapter 3 describes the login procedure and how to enter or change your secret password.

User Categories

The first category of user is the file owner, the person who created a file. The owner of a file can grant *access permissions* for this file to any or all of the three categories of users.

The second category is a member of the file owner's group. A group is simply a set of users who are all granted the same level of access to the same set of files.

The third category of user is everyone else. A user that is neither the owner of the file nor a member of a group that has been granted access rights to that file falls into the third category.

Access Permissions

There are three types of access permissions: read, write, and execute. *Read* permission allows you to examine the contents of a text file. *Write* permission permits you to change or delete a file. *Execute* permission gives you the right to execute a command file. A file owner may grant one or more of these permissions, in any combination, to members of one or more of the three user categories.

For example, the owner of a shell script (an important type of file that contains the sequence of commands executed by the shell) may grant read, write, and execute, permission to himself or herself. The owner may then go on to grant read and execute permission to the members of a group that must be able to use the script, but not change it. Finally, the owner may decide to grant only read permission to everyone else.

Determining Current Permissions in Force

The permissions in force for the files in a directory can be displayed by using the long form of the **ls** command (**ls -l**). A typical directory listing might look similar to the following display:

```
$ ls -l
-rwxr-xr-x  1 allen    other    3399   Apr 26    05:59  active
-rw-r-----  1 allen    other     919   Jul 13    22:40  memo27
drwxr-xr-x  3 allen    root       64   Jul  7    22:21  vpix
$
```

The first ten character positions of the directory listing indicate file permissions. The first character tells you whether the file is a directory or not. If the first character is a **d**, the file is a directory. A dash (−) indicates that the file is not a directory.

The next nine characters are divided into three sets of three. A letter (r, w, or x for read, write, or execute, respectively) denotes that a particular permission has been granted. A dash in the same position shows that that permission has *not* been granted. The first set tells you which permissions the owner of the file has. The second set tells you which permissions other users in the owner's group have. The third set indicates which permissions all other users have.

In the preceding example, the file **active** is not a directory, and it can be read, written, and executed by the file owner. Other users, both in the owner's group and outside it, may read and execute the file, but may not modify it. The file **memo27** may be both read and written by the file owner, may be read by other users in the owner's group, but may not be accessed at all by other users. The third file in this directory, **vpix**, is itself a directory. It may be read from and written to by the directory owner, and he may also execute the program files in the directory. Other users, both within and outside the owner's group, may read and execute files in the directory, but may not modify them.

A user who does not have execute permission for a directory file will not be allowed to change to that directory with the **cd** command. Such a user is thus prevented from accessing any of the files in that directory.

THE SUPERUSER

There is another person who can access and also change the access permissions of any file, regardless of its ownership. This *superuser* has tremendous power, and therefore must be very careful.

The superuser may log in only from the system console, under the user name of **root.** Generally, only the system administrator may log in as **root,** and does so only when the unique power of the superuser is needed.

Only the superuser can add new users to the system and assign them their initial passwords. This person can also retrieve password-protected files when a user leaves the organization without telling someone his or her password.

The superuser is by definition the most trusted individual that uses a Unix system. He or she always has permission to access any file. To use an analogy, being the superuser is like being the manager of an office building and having the master key. The superuser can enter any "room" at any time (though normally would not). If a "tenant skips town," the superuser can "repossess" the abandoned rooms. The superuser can also help the user who has forgotten his "key" (password) regain access to his files.

Chapter 13 will go into more detail about the responsibilities and prerogatives of the system administrator.

MULTIUSER COMMANDS

A number of Unix commands pertain specifically to the multiuser nature of the system. The most important ones are listed in table 9-1 and are briefly discussed in this chapter.

Table 9-1. Multiuser commands

COMMAND	FUNCTION
who	Displays the names of all users currently logged into the system and the time they logged in.
who am i	Displays the name of the user who logged in at the terminal where this command is issued
whodo	Lists each active user's device ID, processes being run, and CPU minutes and seconds used.
id	Returns the user ID and group ID of the user currently logged in. Similar to **who am i.**
su	Allows a user to log in as another user without first logging out. The person issuing the command must know the other user's password.
chmod	Alters the access permissions for a file or directory.
chown	Changes the ownership of a file or directory.
chgrp	Changes the group to which a file or directory belongs.
write	A device for real-time dialogue between two active users.
wall	Broadcasts a message to all active users.

Identifying Users

The **who** command displays a list of who is currently active on the system, at which terminal they are logged in, and the date and time that they logged in. A typical display would be similar to the following:

```
$ who
allen       tty01        Aug 19 14:11
scott       tty03        Aug 19 15:03
pam         tty02        Aug 19 15:17
$
```

The **who am i** command provides the same listing, but only for the user making the request. It is useful if you come upon an active, but unattended terminal and want to find out who is logged in there:

```
$ who am i
allen        tty01        Aug 19 14:11
$
```

The **id** command displays the user ID and group ID of the user issuing the command. The following is an example of using the id command:

```
$ id
uid=201(allen) gid=50(group)
$
```

Changing Your User ID

The **su** command allows an active user to log in temporarily as either the superuser or some other user. If you have several processes going and find you need to perform an operation that only the superuser is allowed to do, you need not log out. Just issue the **su** command with no arguments. After finishing the activity that required you to change identity, you can return to your original login by issuing the **exit** command as follows:

```
$ su
Password:
# who am i
allen        tty01        Aug 19 14:11
# exit
$ who am i
allen        tty01        Aug 19 14:11
$
```

Note the pound sign (#) prompt after the execution of the **su** command, indicating you became the superuser. Even though you used the **su** command to log in as **root,** the system still knows you by your original login name. Exiting the superuser shell returns you to your original login shell, as the dollar sign ($) prompt indicates.

Changing File Access Permissions

Normally, when a user creates a file, read and write access is given to the owner, while read access is given to both group members and others.

With the **chmod** command, the owner of a file can either add or remove permissions. Syntax is shown in figure 9-1.

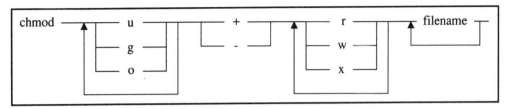

*Figure 9-1. Syntax for the **chmod** command*

The diagram shows that the **chmod** command has four arguments. The first tells whether the command applies to the owner or primary user (u), the user's group (g), or others (o). You can change the permissions for one, two, or all three user categories with a single **chmod** command. This is indicated by the return arrow encircling the three options.

The second argument (+ or –) specifies whether permissions are being added or deleted. The third argument (r, w, or x) designates the permission(s) being changed. Again, the return arrow shows that you can change more than one permission with a single command.

There should be no blank spaces between the first three arguments, but you must leave a space between the third and fourth arguments. The fourth argument is the name of the file or files whose permissions are being changed. Multiple files may be listed here. The same changes will be made to the permissions of all listed files.

Using the example in figure 9-1, table 9-2 shows the effects of using various **chmod** commands.

*Table 9-2. Sample **chmod** commands*

COMMAND	RESULT
chmod go+w *	Grants write permission to file owner's group members and others for all files in the directory.
chmod u-w active	Removes write permission from the primary user (you) for the file named **active**.
chmod o+rw memo27	Grants read and write permission to users outside your group for the file named **memo27**.

For a detailed discussion of the assignment of permission levels, refer to the description of the **chmod** command in the user reference guide that came with your Unix system.

Changing the File Owner

/VIP

The **chown** command allows a file's owner or the superuser to reassign the ownership of that file. Similarly, the **chgrp** command allows the file's owner or the superuser to reassign the group ownership to another group. To transfer a file you own to another user in another group, execute **chgrp** first. If you execute **chown** first, you will no longer be the owner of the file, and thus unable to change its group. Once you have changed the group and owner of a file, you will probably want to copy it into the new owner's directory. To do so, you need read, write, and execute access to that directory.

/VIP

In the following example, a series of commands transfers the file **testfile2** from the user **allen** in the group **group** to the user **joyce** in the group **sales**:

```
login: joyce
Password:
$ chmod go+rwx /usr/joyce
$ exit
login : allen
Password:
$ pwd
/usr/allen
$ ls -l testfile2
-rw-r--r--  1 allen   group    301 Aug 04 17:43 testfile2
$ cp testfile2 /usr/joyce
$ chgrp sales /usr/joyce/testfile2
$ chown joyce /usr/joyce/testfile2
$ cd /usr/joyce
$ ls -l testfile2
-rw-r--r--  1 joyce   sales    301 Aug 19 22:58 testfile2
$
```

The file's owner and group have been changed, and the date and time have been updated. If desired, the original copy of the file can now be removed from **/usr/allen.**

Sending Messages to Other Active Users

With the **write** command, you can establish communication with any other user currently active on the system. After your target user receives your first transmission, he or she can also enter a **write** command to establish a two-way link. At this point you can send a message, terminated with some mutually agreed-upon signal such as *o* for "over." Your coworker can then type a message back to you, again terminated with an *o*. The conversation may continue as long as desired. After both of you agree that the dialogue is concluded (by sending *oo* for "over and out"), you can terminate the link by pressing [Ctrl-d].

In addition to sending messages two ways with the **write** command, it is possible to broadcast a one-way message to all active users with the **wall** command, (derived from **w**ritten to **all** users). The superuser may use it to warn active users of an imminent shutdown of the system. To protect their files, all users are encouraged to log out before the shutdown. If the system is shut down while a user's files are still open, those files could become corrupted.

Users can suppress the display of messages sent by most other users by issuing the **mesg** command. However, the **mesg** command cannot prevent a message from the superuser from being displayed.

PRINT SPOOLING

The Unix print subsystem, **lp**, coordinates the printing of multiple print jobs initiated by multiple users. One or more queues are established, each associated with a class of printer. A large installation may have several letter-quality printers and several high-speed draft-quality printers. The queue linked with the letter-quality printers will always route the top job on the queue to the first available printer of that class. The first job waiting on the draft-quality queue will go to the first available draft printer.

The print queues enable Unix to handle several print jobs at once without confusing them. After you issue an **lp** command and your job is placed on the appropriate print queue, control returns to you. You can proceed to issue additional commands without having to wait for your print job to be completed. The spooler operates in the background and will run your job when it comes to the top of the queue.

The print subsystem, named **lp**, is highly generalized and flexible. Nearly all applications make use of it, rather than attempting to send output directly to the printer.

ACTIVITY LOGS

One of the responsibilities of the system administrator is to see that system resources are used efficiently and that all users receive the same high level of service. To do so, you must have sufficient information on system utilization. You may maintain logs of system activity to tell you whether any users are consuming excessive CPU time or excessive memory or are staying logged in too long. The logs can also tell you what commands each user is executing. From this information, you can deduce whether the activity you see for a particular user is appropriate.

The default situation is for this *process accounting* to be turned off. On a busy system, activity logs can grow rapidly, using up valuable hard-disk space. If you want to use process accounting, you must pay close attention to it. Turn accounting on, record the data you want, then turn it off.

An alternative is to monitor closely the sizes of the accounting files. When they reach a certain predetermined size, clean them out and start over.

On a system with only a few users, where resources are seldom or never stretched to the limit, you may never want to turn accounting on. On a system with a relatively large number of users, however, the process-accounting logs provide a valuable tool in the perpetual quest for optimal system performance.

The process-accounting logs vary from one Unix system to another, but some features are common to all. The **accton** command turns the accounting logs on and off. The log used most frequently is the current-process accounting file, usually named **/usr/adm/pacct**. This file contains a list of every command executed by the system. Along with the command name, it records the user name, terminal name, start time, end time, real time used, CPU time used, and average amount of RAM used. The **acctcom** command will display the contents of this file on standard output.

SUMMARY

Because Unix was designed as a multiuser system, it requires structures not needed in a single-user operating system such as DOS. One multiuser structure designed for security purposes is the login and password system. Another is the requirement for a superuser to maintain the entire system. In a context where different people are invested with different levels of trust, there must be one person who is completely trusted. That person is the system administrator, who is known as the superuser when logged in as **root**.

Under Unix, a user can be separately granted permission to read, change, or execute a particular file. Users are divided into three categories with respect to any one file. These three categories help maintain file security by affording three levels of access permission. The file's owner has one, usually the highest, level of access permission. Every user is also assigned membership in one or more groups of users that have common interests. When a user creates a file, other users in the same group inherit the group level of access permission. Users who are neither the owner nor in the owner's group receive the third level of access permission. Any of these three categories can receive anywhere from full read/write/execute access to no access whatsoever. The superuser always has permission to access any file.

A number of Unix commands are specifically designed to help users work in a multiuser environment. Some allow a user to determine who is active on the system and, if desired, to communicate with other users. Others allow a file owner to change access permissions as well as file ownership.

The system of spooling print jobs onto queues provides for the orderly production of printed output, even when multiple users are trying to obtain printouts at the same time. The only way to guarantee that one user's print job will not interfere with another is to use the **lp** command.

The system administrator can track system usage by examining one or more of the activity logs that are maintained by a Unix system. If an error occurs, the activity log can often help pinpoint the source of the problem. Users that are misusing system resources can also be identified.

Chapter 10

Process Management

Processes are programs in a state of execution. Unix supports multiple simultaneous processes. Each user can run one foreground process and several background processes from a single terminal. When a user logs in, a process that runs the shell program is started. An executing process can launch a new process while it continues to run. The original process is called the *parent*, and the new process is called the *child*.

Handwritten margin notes:
system call
fork
exec
wait
signals # kill -9, 369
ptrace
pipe

LAUNCHING A NEW PROCESS

The shell provides a good example of this phenomenon. When you issue a command to the shell, in most cases the shell starts a new process that executes the command. The shell waits until the new process runs to completion, then reassumes control, using the **fork** and the **exec** system calls.

These operations are generally invisible to both the typical user and the applications programmer. However, it is helpful to understand what is going on beneath the surface of the shell user interface.

The fork System Call

An active process can clone itself by issuing the **fork** system call. The resulting child process executes the exact same program as the parent and has the same open files. However, the two processes have different process ID numbers and different parent process ID numbers. Figure 10-1 on the next page shows the activity of the parent and child processes as a function of time. Note that at any given instant, only one process is active. Cloning a process is useful because the child process can be changed to run a different program.

The exec System Call

The **exec** system call allows an active program to chain to another program. The files that were open for the original program remain open for the new one, and the new program becomes the active one. By issuing **fork** followed by **exec**, one process can spawn a second process that runs a different program and, upon completion, sends the results back to the parent process. Figure 10-2 shows a **fork** followed by an **exec** diagramed as a function of time.

The wait System Call

At some point, a parent process may need to suspend execution until it receives a result back from one of its children. This situation occurs, for example, when the shell spawns a process to run a command. In such cases, the **wait** system call is executed, causing the parent process to be suspended until the child process is either completed or "dies." This saves wasting system cycles on a process that is only idling while waiting for the occurrence of an event.

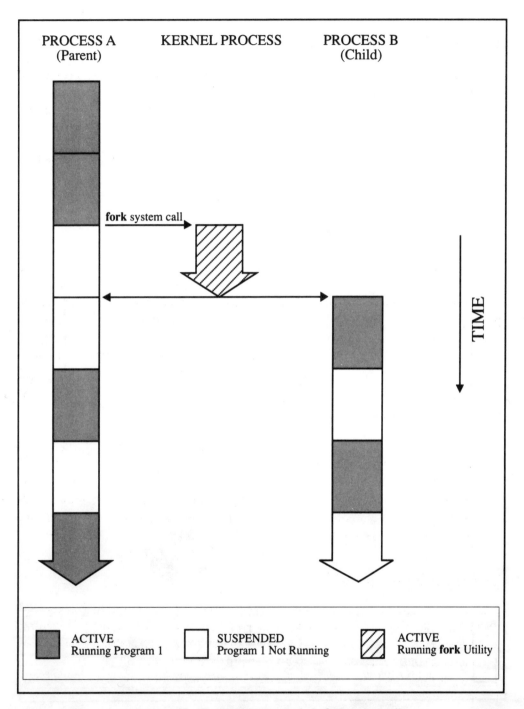

PROCESS A   KERNEL PROCESS   PROCESS B
(Parent)   (Child)

fork system call

TIME

| | ACTIVE
Running Program 1 | | SUSPENDED
Program 1 Not Running | | ACTIVE
Running **fork** Utility |

*Figure 10-1. Cloning a process with the **fork** system call*

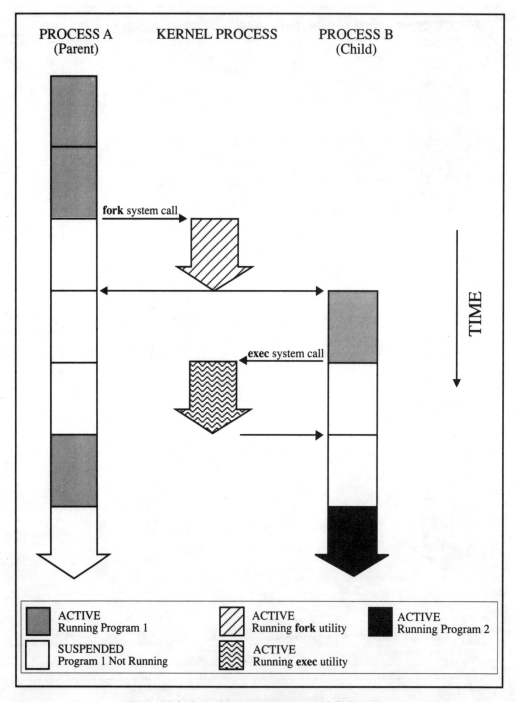

Figure 10-2. Launching a new process with fork and exec

For example, when the shell launches a foreground process, it also issues a **wait** system call. This causes the shell to suspend operation until the child process, which it created, dies.

VIP

When launching a background process, the shell does not issue a **wait**. The shell prompt returns to the terminal immediately, and you may enter another command while the background process continues to execute.

 # nice.

ALTERING PROCESS PRIORITY

Of several processes running simultaneously, some are probably more time-critical than others. For example, you probably want your foreground task to finish as quickly as possible. Some of your background tasks may not be so urgent. You can organize your processes by setting a *priority* for each one. A higher-priority process will be given more CPU cycles and thus will run faster than a lower-priority process.

VIP

All users may lower the priority of their own processes by issuing the **nice** command. A "nice" process will altruistically give up CPU cycles so that other processes can have more. Only the superuser has the power to use the **nice** command to raise the priority of a process. This prevents a greedy user from selfishly taking system resources at the expense of others.

If you are running processes in the background and don't immediately need their results, consider lowering their priorities with the **nice** command. Your own foreground process and the processes of other users will run a little faster. The first argument of the **nice** command is the number of priority units being surrendered, and the second argument is the command whose priority is being changed. For example, to lower the priority of a command that searches all the files in the current directory for the character string "education," use the following command line:

-15 - # of priority

```
$ nice -15 grep education * > education.out &
```

decrease priority

The priority of the background **grep** command is reduced by 15 priority units.

The superuser could *increase* the priority of the same command as follows:

```
$ nice --15 grep education * > education.out &
```

↑ increase priority

The double minus sign indicates that priority is to increase by 15 units. *VIP*

note: Don't use "nice" cmnd in forgrnd job. You Can get locked

LOGGING OUT WHILE A BACKGROUND PROCESS IS STILL RUNNING

Normally, when a user logs out, all of that user's processes, including background processes, are immediately terminated. Sometimes, however, you may want to allow a background process to continue executing after you have logged out for the day. To do this, use the **nohup** command (derived from **no hangup**). Syntax for the **nohup** command is simple. It has only one argument, which is the command you wish to protect. For example, to protect the **grep** command in the preceding example, use the following syntax:

```
$ nohup grep education * > education.out &
```

Execution will continue until the task is finished, even if you log out before then.

Note that if you want to protect a command pipeline from premature termination, every element in the pipeline must contain the **nohup** command. If even one element does not have a **nohup**, that element will be terminated when you log out, destroying the entire pipeline in the process.

INTERPROCESS COMMUNICATION

In Unix's multitasking operating environment, multiple tasks or processes may execute simultaneously. These processes may be initiated by a single user or by multiple users. In either case, it is often useful for such processes to communicate with each other. Several mechanisms permit such interprocess communication.

Signals

The signal is the simplest form of interprocess communication. There are 22 different signals (see table 10-1).These carry no information other than their presence.

Only an active process can send a signal to another process. Since only one process can be active at any given instant, the destination process must be suspended. When the destination process "wakes up," the kernel checks to see whether any signals have arrived for it. If so, one of three actions occurs: the signal is passed through to the destination, it is ignored, or it is caught (meaning a special signal-handling routine is run).

Table 10-1. Signals and their meanings ≈ *interopt*

NUMBER	NAME	MEANING
01	SIGHUP	hangup
02	SIGINT	interrupt
03	SIGQUIT	quit and produce a core dump
04	SIGILL	illegal instruction
05	SIGTRAP	trace trap
06	SIGIOT	IOT instruction
07	SIGABRT	abort
08	SIGEMT	EMT instruction
09	SIGKILL	kill (cannot be caught or ignored)
10	SIGBUS	bus error
11	SIGSEGV	segmentation violation
12	SIGSYS	bad argument in system call
13	SIGPIPE	data was put into a dead-end pipe
14	SIGALRM	alarm clock
15	SIGTERM	software termination signal
16	SIGUSR1	user-defined signal #1
17	SIGUSR2	user-defined signal #2
18	SIGCLD	death of a child
19	SIGPWR	power fail
20	unspecified	
21	unspecified	
22	SIGPOLL	selectable event pending

One of the most commonly used signals is signal 15, the software termination signal. It politely asks the destination process to commit suicide. A process may be set up so that it will ignore signal 15 and continue to run. However, signal 9, the kill signal, cannot be ignored. When a process receives the kill signal, it must cease running immediately.

Signals are sent with the **kill** command. This command is poorly named because it can send 20 other signals besides the one for terminating a process. An example of its use would be as follows:

```
$ kill -9 369
```

The command in this example shuts down process number 369. Naturally, you would use the **kill** command only to terminate a background process. (You can halt the foreground process by pressing [ctrl-c].) If you do not specify a signal number, signal 15 is assumed.

Process Tracing

Another form of interprocess communication occurs between a parent and its child. It is normally used to debug the code of the child process. The parent issues a **ptrace** system call. Execution of the child proceeds until it receives a signal. At that point the child stops, allowing the parent to examine or change the child's internal code. The child may then resume executing or terminate.

Pipes

As explained in chapter 6, a *pipe* is a conduit that allows information to flow from the standard output of one process to the standard input of another. Sometimes a pipe is called a FIFO (first in first out) because the first byte of information that goes into the pipe is also the first byte that comes out. Like **ptrace, pipe** is a system call that you would normally include in a C program.

The following command line, when executed, will display the names of files in the current directory in alphabetical order:

```
$ ls | sort
```

The output of the **ls** process is piped to the input of the **sort** process, whose output is then displayed on the terminal screen.

This example illustrates one of the limitations of *ordinary* pipes. Both processes connected by the pipe are children of the same parent, which in this case is the user shell. Ordinary pipes can send information from one process to another only if they have the same parent. This is because ordinary pipes are created within the context of a parent process, and they die when the parent dies.

Named pipes are structured differently. They appear as special files in the **/dev** directory, along with disk drives and printers. Functionally, named pipes operate just like ordinary pipes, but they may connect processes that have different parents.

Queues (очередность)   First in First out

Queues, also called the IPC Message Facility, provide another method of sharing information between processes. A queue is an area of main memory that is shared by a sending process and a receiving process. Multiple sending processes may place messages on the queue, and multiple receiving processes may read these messages. Queues are FIFO constructions. The first message placed on a queue will be the first one read.

First in First out

A common application for a queue is the print-spooling function. Multiple processes may place print jobs on the spooler queue, and multiple printers may take those jobs off the queue. The first job placed on the queue will be the first one printed by the first available printer.

Shared Memory

In memory sharing, a block of data is sent via a portion of main memory from one process to another. Queues represent one form of memory sharing; a more generalized form of shared memory is also available. You can set aside an area of main memory to be used as shared memory. By using system calls, active processes can read or write data in that area. As soon as one process writes information into shared memory, the data become available to all other processes. Figure 10-3 is a partial memory map showing how shared memory is used.

Semaphores

You can probably see some potential problems with shared memory. What if two processes attempt to update the same place in shared memory at the same time? Corruption of data could result. Semaphores prevent this problem. By setting a semaphore with a system call, one process can prevent other processes from affecting shared memory until it is finished with its own update. By serializing operations that would otherwise occur in parallel, semaphores protect the integrity of the system.

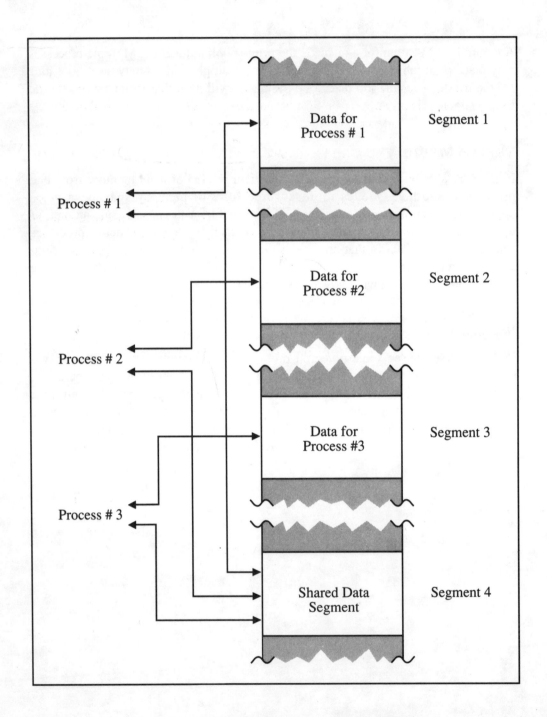

Figure 10-3. Shared memory used by three processes

SUMMARY

One of the key features of the Unix operating system is that it is able to execute multiple jobs concurrently. To do this, it launches a process for each job, then divides up the system's resources among the processes.

The operation of processes can be affected by various system calls, which are low-level programming constructs not available from the shell.

Each terminal on a Unix system can support one foreground process and multiple background processes. By changing the priority levels of active processes, you can control how quickly each will run. You can give preference to processes whose results are urgently needed at the expense of processes whose output is not immediately needed.

There is a wide variety of mechanisms for sharing information among active processes. Information sharing increases the value of multitasking. Not only does it reduce total execution time for all jobs, but the sharing of information between related processes allows greater flexibility in the way an application may be coded.

Chapter 11

Communications

One of the great strengths of Unix is its provision for communication among users. Users on a single Unix system may communicate not only among themselves but also with users on other Unix systems. Systems may be connected by a local area network (LAN), wide area network (WAN), or telephone modem.

Of course, on a stand-alone DOS system, local communication is not possible, since DOS is a single-user operating system. Remote communication is possible over a network or modem.

LOCAL COMMUNICATION

Unix provides for various forms of local communication. A message may be either broadcast to all users that are active when it is sent or directed to one or more specific users.

Broadcast Messages

Broadcast communications are sent from one user to all other users on the system. There are three forms of broadcast communication: news, message of the day, and write to all users. News and message of the day can be sent only by the superuser, but any user can broadcast a message with the **wall** (write-to-**all**) command.

News items are stored in the **/usr/news** directory. In addition, a file named **.news time** in each user's home directory keeps track of the last time that user read the news. When you issue the **news** command, all news items that were created after the last time you read the news (that is, the current news items) will be displayed. By using the **-a** option with the **news** command, you can display all news items, whether they are current or not.

The message of the day is broadcast by the superuser to all users when they log in. When a user logs in, the files **/etc/profile** and **/usr/.profile** are executed. The **.etc/profile** file contains the command **cat /etc/motd**, and the file **motd** displays the message of the day. The system administrator may change the contents of **motd** as often as desired, but should be aware that if a message is left in for too long, users will get tired of seeing it and will start ignoring the message of the day altogether.

The **wall** command broadcasts a message to all users. Usually, the system administrator is the only person who needs to communicate the same message to all users. However, the **wall** command may be used by anyone.

Private Messages

As explained in chapter 9, the **write** command provides a form of two-way communication between two active users. After you have established contact with your destination, each line of text that you type is sent individually when you press the [Enter] key. You and your correspondent can engage in a dialogue by alternately typing messages to each other. The conversation will be terminated when you both type [Ctrl-d] or type a period (.) as the first character of a new line.

The **mesg** command gives a user the option of rejecting incoming messages created by either the **write** or the **wall** command. If a user issues the command **mesg n**, all incoming messages will be refused; they will not be displayed on the screen. To reinstate the acceptance of messages, issue the **mesg y** command.

The `mail` Command

The **mail** command is the most powerful and popular tool for communicating with other users on a stand-alone system; it is also useful for communicating with users on remote systems. The electronic-mail system allows you to send messages to other users whether they are currently logged in or not. Each user has his or her own personal mailbox to which mail messages are routed. The mail can be read at any time that is convenient to the recipient.

To send a quick message to another user, simply enter the **mail** command with the user's login ID, then start typing your message. When you are finished, type [Ctrl-d]. Your message will immediate ly appear in the addressee's mailbox. For example, the following is a message from Allen to Joyce:

```
$ mail joyce
Subject: Finance committee meeting
This week's meeting of the finance committee has been rescheduled
to Friday at 2:30 in the afternoon. Please come prepared to
defend your departmental budget. -- Allen
(end of message)
```

Reading your own mail is even easier. Just issue the **mail** command with no arguments. The titles of all the messages in your mailbox will be displayed on the screen. You can select which ones you want to read. For example, Joyce's mailbox might look like the following:

```
$ mail
mail version 3.0 January 28,1987.  Type ? for help.
2 messages:
     2 allen  Thu Mar 22 21:10  10/338 "Finance committee meeting"
     1 root   Sat Mar 17 21:25  10/231 "Welcome to xenix 386"
2
Message  2:
From allen Thu Mar 22 21:10:23 1990
To: joyce
Subject: Finance committee meeting
Date: Thu Mar 22 21:10:23 1990
This week's meeting of the finance committee has been rescheduled
to Friday at 2:30 in the afternoon.  Please come prepared to
defend your departmental budget. -- Allen
-
```

The mail system is now waiting for you to enter one of the mail commands. To delete the message you have just read, issue the **d** command. You can undelete a deleted message with the **u** command, as long as you do so before quitting **mail** with the **q** command. Once you return to the shell, any mail messages that you have deleted are gone forever. If you leave the mail system by issuing the **x** (exit) command rather than the **q** (quit) command, all mail will be put back into your mailbox unchanged. Deletions will not take effect.

After reading a message, but before deleting it, you have the opportunity to save it to a file for future reference. The **s** command or the **y** command will perform the save operation. If you do not specify a destination file name, the system will place it in a file named **mbox**. You can also use the **lpr** command to print any of your messages. Keep your mailbox as clean as possible so that new messages receive prompt attention. You should, therefore, delete messages from your mailbox after you have saved them to another file or printed them.

COMMUNICATION BETWEEN UNIX SYSTEMS

There are compelling reasons for establishing communication between computer systems. Most of them have to do with the sharing of resources. One system may have peripheral devices, databases, or programs that are needed by the user of a less well endowed system. Both DOS and Unix support networking to provide resource sharing, and also to let users on different systems communicate with each other. The systems on the network, called *nodes*, may be confined to a local area (with a LAN), or they may be located anywhere in the world (communicating via a WAN).

Unix possesses a rich set of network-support features. Networking has been much more common in the Unix community than in the DOS world and has been established for a much longer time. The primary mechanism Unix uses for communicating with other computer systems is the **uucp** data-transfer system. Table 11-1 shows the most important commands associated with the **uucp** system and describes their functions.

Table 11-1. Common Unix networking commands

COMMAND	FUNCTION
cu	Allows a local Unix user to call and log into another system. The remote system may or may not be Unix-based.
uucp	Copies files both ways between the local system and a remote Unix system.
uulog	Displays selected entries in the log of file-copy activity.
uuname	Displays a list of names of all remote systems known to the local **uucp** system.
uupick	Allows a user to accept or reject a file that has been sent to the local **/usr/spool/uucppublic/receive** directory by a remote system.
uustat	Reports the status of or kills a previously issued **uucp** command.
uuto	Sends a file to the **/usr/spool/uucppublic/receive** directory of a remote system.
uux	Allows a user on one Unix system to execute a command on a remote Unix system.
uuxqt	Local program that enables the execution of a command called for by a remote **uux** command.

The cu Command

The **cu** command allows your terminal to emulate another to make use of the **uucp** control files. With it you can talk to other Unix systems, DOS systems, bulletin boards, or anything else that has an asynchronous ASCII port. You can even connect with an IBM mainframe through an appropriate protocol converter.

To establish a connection, you need to specify only the name of a known remote computer. The **uucp** control files contain all other necessary information, such as type of connection, transmission speed, and telephone number. For example, to communicate with a remote system named **dolphin**, you would use the following syntax:

```
$ cu dolphin
```

Alternatively, you can specify the telephone number of the remote system if you have an autodial modem attached to your system and the destination system is similarly equipped:

```
$ cu 5553220
```

A minus sign (–) inserted into the number will introduce a delay of several seconds, and an equals sign (=) will wait for a secondary dial tone. You may have to experiment with one or both of these characters until you find a sequence that works consistently with the remote computer you wish to call.

Once the **cu** command establishes a connection, your screen will display:

```
$ cu dolphin
Connected
```

At this point, you can type in text that will be sent to the remote system, receive data from the remote system, or perform one of the special **cu** subcommands. All **cu** subcommands begin with the tilde (~) character and are defined in table 11-2.

For the **cu** subcommands to succeed, the remote system must be waiting at the PS1 prompt. The **cu** command is able to transfer only ASCII files, and does not do any error checking. You should check received files with the **wc** (word count) command to verify that the number of words received is the same as the number of words sent. To transfer binary files, it is better to use either **uuto** or **uucp**.

The uuto Command

The **uuto** command uses the **uucp** control files to send files from the local system to a remote system. For security reasons, you cannot use **uuto** to write files to any desired directory on the remote system. This command will, by default, write files to the directory **/usr/spool/uucppublic/receive**. From there, the destination user on the remote system can retrieve the files with the **uupick** command. Consider the following example:

```
$ uuto -m matchmate360 matchmate1200 dolphin!saleem
```

In this example, the two files, **matchmate360** and **matchmate1200**, are sent to a user whose login name is **saleem** on a remote system named **dolphin**. The last argument of the command is always the destination system and user, joined by the bang (!) character. The arguments immediately preceding the destination are the names of the files to be transferred. Options may also be specified; if they are used, they always precede any other arguments, and they always start with a minus sign (–). In the above example, the **-m** option instructs the remote system to send an electronic-mail message to Saleem to inform him of the arrival of the files.

*Table 11-2. List of **cu** commands*

COMMAND	FUNCTION
~	Terminate the connection.
~!	Escape temporarily to a local subshell.
~!command	Run command on the local system.
~$command	Run command on the local system, but send its output to the remote system.
~%cd newdir	Change the directory on the local system.
~%take fromfile tofile	Copy a file named **fromfile** on the remote system to a file named **tofile** on the local system. If you do not wish to change the name of the file, omit the **tofile** argument.
~%put fromfile tofile	Copy a file named **fromfile** on the local system to a file named **tofile** on the remote system. If you do not wish to change the name of the file, omit the **tofile** argument.
~%break	Transmit a **break** command to the remote system.
~%debug	Toggle the debugging option on or off.
~~command	Send a tilde command to be executed by the copy of **cu** running on the remote machine.
~t	Display values of termio structure variables for the user's terminal (for debug purposes). Termio is the general terminal interface.
~l	Display values of remote communication line's termio structure variables (for debug purposes).
~%nostop	Toggles on and off DC3/DC1 input control.

The receiver can now use the **uupick** command to transfer all, some (or none) of the files to another directory. The **uupick** command also permits scanning the contents of each file before deciding on its disposition. After reviewing and transferring files, the receiver should delete them from the public directory to keep it from becoming cluttered.

The uucp Command

The **uucp** command is a considerably more powerful file-transfer mechanism than **uuto**. With the **uucp** command, you can copy a file from a remote system to your local system, as well as vice versa. Also, **uucp** can copy files into a specified directory on the remote system, rather than only to **/usr/spool/uucppublic/receive**.

For example, to copy the file **matchmate360** from the current directory on the local system to Saleem's home directory on the **dolphin** system, use the following command line:

```
$ uucp matchmate360 dolphin!~saleem
```

You can even copy files from one remote system to another. The syntax would be similar to the following:

```
$ uucp dolphin!~saleem/matchmate360 orca!~fred/externaldisk
```

In this example, a file named **matchmate360** is copied from Saleem's home directory on the **dolphin** system to Fred's home directory on the **orca** system. In the process, the name of the file is changed to **externaldisk**.

The power of the **uucp** system also makes it a potentially dangerous tool. The **uucp** command is able to retrieve files from, as well as write files to, remote computers. The **uux** command can execute programs on remote computers. Together, these capabilities threaten the privacy of files and even make Unix systems susceptible to the misappropriation or destruction of programs and data. Therefore, most system administrators severely restrict what a remote user can do with the **uucp** system. You will find there are some operations you are allowed to perform on one remote system but not on another. What is allowed on a specific system is controlled by the contents of a file named **/usr/lib/uucp/Permissions**.

The uux Command

The **uux** command is even more powerful (and thus potentially more dangerous) than the **uucp** command. With **uux**, you can gather files from several remote machines and execute a command using the files on another remote machine. Consider this command line:

```
$ uux "cat sys1!/usr/joe/part1 sys2!/usr/fred/part2 > !/usr/allen/memo"
```

In this example, a file named **part1** is taken from Joe's directory on system **sys1** and is concatenated with a file named **part2** from Fred's directory on system **sys2**. The concatenation command is executed on the local system, and the result is redirected to a file named **memo** in Allen's directory on the local system. The command line is quoted to prevent the shell from interpreting the greater-than sign (>) before the **uux** command is executed.

If the command argument of a **uux** command is a pipeline, only the first segment of the pipe may specify a machine. The **uux** command requires that all parts of a pipeline be executed on the same machine. If a **uux** command fails for any reason, it sends a mail message to the user who issued the command.

The uustat Command

The **uucp** commands do not return any indication of successful completion to the user who issues them. To check the status of such tasks, use the **uustat** command. It performs several functions, depending on the options selected, but its primary purpose is to report to you the status of your **uucp** tasks that have been queued, but not yet completed. If you issue one or more **uucp** commands followed by a **uustat** command, and the **uustat** command returns no output, it means that all the **uucp** commands have been successfully completed. Any transactions that have not yet been completed will be displayed.

For example, if you sent the file **testfile1** to the user **joyce** on the system **system2**, followed immediately by a **uustat** command, the result would be:

```
$ uuto testfile1 system2!joyce
$ uustat
system2N70d3  08/28-16:05  S  system2  allen 301 /usr/allen/testfile1
$
```

The display shows the job ID, date and time, an **S** signifying the message is to be sent (**R** would signify the message is to be received), the name of the target system, the login ID of the local user, the file size in bytes (301), and the name and path of the file to be transferred.

The -**a** option displays all jobs waiting in the **uucp** queue, regardless of who originated them. The -**q** option indicates why each job is still in the queue. For example, the following display indicates that one command file is waiting because no communications device is currently available on **system2**:

```
$ uuto testfile1 system2!joyce
$ uustat -q
system2    1C           08/28-16:05 NO DEVICES AVAILABLE
$
```

The **uustat** command can also be used to kill a job in the queue. Use the **-k** option along with the job ID of the **uucp** request that you want to abort. The display for this operation will be similar to the following:

```
$ uustat -ksystem2N70d3
Job: system2N70d3 successfully killed
$
```

Note that there is no blank space between the -k option and the job ID.

You can also use **uustat** to check the queue status of any specified remote system or the queue status for any specified local user.

The uulog Command

The **uulog** command displays the contents of a log file that keeps track of all **uucp** jobs that have been queued. In the following example, the log entry identifies the transaction and indicates whether it was successful or not:

```
$ uulog
uucp system2  (8/28-16:05:41,549,0) CONN FAILED
(NO DEVICES AVAILABLE)
$
```

A separate log file is kept for each remote system in the directory **/usr/spool/uucp/.Log/uucico** or the directory **/usr/spool/uucp/.Log/uuxqt**.

TCP/IP   QNX use TCP/IP com. system

As a networking system, **uucp** has a number of significant advantages. It works equally well for local-area networks and for wide-area networks connected by telephone lines. Also, it does not require any special hardware. Ordinary, low-cost, RS-232 links serve as connections for local networks. Inexpensive telephone modems allow access to other systems around the world.

For many users, **uucp** is all the communication capability they will ever need. However, it does have some deficiencies. One major drawback is speed. Most RS-232 links operate at anywhere from 1200 to 9600 baud, which is about 1200 to 9600 bits per second. This is a very low data-transfer rate compared with the internal speed of modern personal computers.

On a LAN, where the speed of modems need not be considered, it is possible to link computers with much higher speed channels. For example, the popular Ethernet has a 10-MHz bandwidth; as many as 10 million bits per second can be transmitted. Even with average data rates of 1 MHz, such networks are over 100 times faster than an RS-232 network.

To establish communication between two systems across a local-area network, the systems need to communicate through an agreed-upon protocol. One of the most popular protocols in the Unix community is called TCP/IP, which stands for Transmission Control Protocol/Internet Protocol. It was developed by and for the U.S. Department of Defense, but has migrated to the general-user community. It is particularly common on Ethernet systems.

SUMMARY

The ability to communicate freely with other users is one of the great strengths of the Unix system. There are two levels of communication: multiple users on a single Unix system sharing system resources and information, and users on different Unix systems communicating with each other over network links.

On an isolated multiuser system, there are several mechanisms that allow the system administrator to communicate with other users. Also, other commands allow users to converse with each other in real time over their terminals and to send electronic mail to others.

When Unix systems are interconnected over a wide-area or local-area network, the **uucp** communication system is most commonly used. It provides for copying files from one system to another, as well as the execution of programs on a remote system by a local user. Other, more powerful communication systems, such as TCP/IP, may be preferable where network performance is a limiting factor.

Chapter 12

Shell Programming

S hell programming in Unix is very similar to batch programming in DOS, but considerably more powerful. Unix has a much larger set of shell commands and flow-control constructs than DOS. In many cases, you will be able to perform a function with a short shell program (called a *script*) that would require a full-blown BASIC or C program in the DOS environment. Consequently, shell programming plays a much more important role in Unix systems than batch programming plays in DOS systems.

This chapter describes the most important Bourne shell features and the most commonly used commands and operators. These constitute only a fraction of the available commands, but they are the ones you are most likely to need. Examples for many commands are given, and in cases where a desired result can be achieved in more than one way, the relative merits of each approach are discussed.

Over the years, different Unix shells have evolved to meet the respective needs of a diverse community of users. Recently, as a result of the efforts to agree on a standard version of Unix, three shells have risen to prominence. The *Bourne shell*, developed by Steve Bourne at AT&T Bell Laboratories, is the standard shell that comes with all versions of Unix endorsed by AT&T. It is the shell used throughout this book for the examples. The *C shell* was developed for the Berkeley versions of Unix. It is similar to the Bourne shell in many respects, but has some additional features. The *Korn shell,* available on some systems, was also developed at AT&T and incorporates some important features of the C shell with additional enhancements to the Bourne shell. Unix System V Release 3.2 and later releases provide both the Bourne shell and the C shell, as does Xenix System V.

BOURNE SHELL BASICS

You will generally use the Bourne shell interactively, entering commands at the shell prompt and examining the results. The principal objects you will work with are *operators, variables,* and *commands.* For some purposes, you may assemble these elements together into scripts. Such scripts are executed just like commands.

Operators, also called *special characters,* change the meaning of other characters that appear with them on a command line. Chapter 6 explained several such special characters: the asterisk (*), the question mark (?), and the brackets ([ ]) are forms of the wildcard character; the less-than (<), greater-than (>), and double-greater-than (>>) are the redirection operators. The special characters covered in this chapter are particularly useful in shell scripts.

Background Processing: the & Operator

Since Unix is a multitasking operating system, it allows you to run multiple jobs simultaneously. If you were to give the computer instructions that let two or more jobs vie for input from the terminal keyboard or try to send output to the terminal screen, confusion would result. To avoid such a situation, you should allow only one job at a time to access a terminal. The job that has access to the terminal is said to be operating in the foreground. All other jobs, which do not communicate with the terminal, are said to be operating in the background.

To run a command or program in the background, you must make sure that it does not interact with the terminal. The usual method is to redirect the input and output to files. The command can thus receive the input it needs, and its output can be retrieved later.

For background processing, you enter a command exactly as you would enter a foreground command, except that you must add an ampersand (&) as the last character on the command line. The shell will create a background process for the execution of this command and return the process number it has assigned to the background process, then display the next shell prompt.

Background processing is useful for time-consuming tasks. Since you can simultaneously work on another task in the foreground, your productivity is increased. You can launch any number of background processes, but, depending on the amount of memory you have installed and the speed of your processor, performance may start to suffer if too many background processes are active at once.

An example of a good candidate for background processing is the **grep** command, which searches a file for a specified pattern (string) of characters. If the file is large, the search may be lengthy. For example, the following command line will cause the system to search for the character string "needle" in the file named **haystack:**

```
$ grep needle haystack > pincushion &
583
$
```

If any instances of the string are found, the lines that contain them are written into the file named **pincushion**. This background process was assigned an ID of 583, then the shell prompt was immediately displayed to enable you to enter another command.

Multiple Commands on a Line: the ; Operator

Normally the carriage return/linefeed (newline) character is the delimiter between commands. When you press [Enter] after typing a command, Unix assumes that your next input will be a new command. However, you may enter multiple commands on the same line by using the semicolon (;) as a delimiter. When the shell sees a semicolon, it assumes that the command it has been reading is now complete and will process the command before proceeding to the material that follows the semicolon.

For example, to change to your home directory, display the name of the directory, then list all files that contain chapters of your book, issue the following command line:

```
$ cd; pwd; ls chapter??
```

The system will respond with the following display:

```
/usr/allen
chapter01
chapter02
chapter03
chapter04
chapter05
chapter06
chapter07
chapter08
```

In this example, three commands, each separated by the semicolon delimiter, were entered on a single line and executed in sequence.

Turning Off the Special Meaning of Special Characters with the \ Operator

Since the metacharacters and other special characters are symbols such as punctuation marks, they also appear in ordinary text. When a command line includes arguments with such symbols used in their nonspecial sense, you need to tell the system to read the characters as ordinary text, not as operators.

The Bourne shell provides several methods. The simplest is the backslash (\). The backslash is a special character whose function is to disable any special meaning that the immediately following character might have, insuring that the character will be read as ordinary text.

For example, consider a case where you want to search through a document for any mention of the monetary amount $500. Since the dollar sign is a special character, the following command will not work:

```
$ grep $500 contract.doc
```

In this example, the dollar sign will be interpreted as a variable substitution operator, not as a dollar sign. The backslash removes the special significance of the dollar sign, as illustrated by the following example:

```
$ grep \$500 contract.doc
```

This command will produce the desired result. Any occurrences of the string "$500" in the file **contract.doc** will be displayed.

Turning Off the Special Meaning of Special Characters with the ' Operator

A pair of apostrophes turns off the special meaning of any characters placed between them. For example, the following command will find all occurrences of the string "$500":

```
$ grep '$500' contract.doc
```

The result will be the same as with the command that incorporated the backslash. The apostrophe is the preferred method if there is more than one special character in an argument or if there are multiple words separated by spaces. Words separated by spaces will be taken as separate arguments unless they are grouped by an operator such as a pair of apostrophes.

The apostrophe operator also affects how variables are treated. Variables are denoted by a preceding dollar sign ($). In the above example, if the argument "$500" were not enclosed in apostrophes, the shell would search the file for a variable named **$500**. Finding none, it would return the shell prompt.

Turning Off the Special Meaning of Special Characters with the " Operator

The double-quote (") operator functions like the apostrophe operator. It is weaker than the apostrophe, however, in that it does not turn off the dollar-sign operator or the grave (`) operator (explained in the following section). Therefore, the *value* of a variable named within a pair of double quotes will be substituted for the *name* of the variable. For example, the following command would not retrieve all instances of the string "$500" from the contract file:

```
$ grep "$500" contract.doc
```

Instead, it would look for a *variable* named **$500** and would find that no such variable had been defined. No output would be returned.

131

Command Substitution Using the ` Operator

Just as a variable substitutes a value for an expression, the grave, or back-quote, operator substitutes the result of a command for an expression. In effect, the grave operator lets you embed one command within another, which is a powerful tool.

In most cases, command substitution is accomplished by setting a variable equal to a command enclosed within back quotes. That variable can then be used as an argument by other commands. For example, to sort a client list named **client.unsort** and display the sorted list on your terminal screen, the following command would be used:

```
$ echo `sort client.unsort`
```

In this example, the **echo** command causes the result of the **sort** command (enclosed within the two graves) to be displayed on the screen.

Summary of Common Special Characters

Table 12-1 lists the most common special characters with a brief description of their function.

Table 12-1. Special characters and their meanings

CHARACTER	FUNCTION
>	Output redirection; sends command output to a file, replacing the current contents of the file.
>>	Output redirection; sends command output to a file, appending it to the current contents of the file.
<	Input redirection; receives command input from a file instead of from standard input.
*	Wildcard; matches any sequence of characters, including the null character.
?	Wildcard; matches any single character, except the null character.
[ ]	Wildcard; matches any of the single characters contained between the brackets.

Table 12-1 (continued)

;	Command delimiter.
&	Indicates background processing of preceding command pipeline.
\	Removes any special meaning from the following character.
'...'	Removes any special meaning from the characters contained between the apostrophes.
"..."	Removes any special meaning from the characters between the quotes, except $ and ` retain their special meanings. Treats all material between the quotes as a single word.
`...`	Returns the output of the command contained between the grave operators. This output can then be used as an argument of another command.
$	Denotes the value of a variable. $HOME is the value of the variable HOME.
|	Pipe; directs the output of one command to the input of a following command.
#	Comment; first character of a comment.
[newline]	Command delimiter; ends a command.
[space]	Argument delimiter; ends an argument or word.

Shell Variables

The Unix shell allows local and global variables, as do most modern programming environments. *Local variables* are accessible only to the shell under which they were created. *Global variables* are called *environment variables* because they are maintained "in the environment." To change a variable from local to environmental, you must export it. Once exported to the environment, a variable can be used by all processes started by the current shell.

Shell variables are able to store only one type of data, the text string. Numeric data is not supported directly, although the **expr** command does give some number manipulation capability.

There are several kinds of variables. The most common is the named variable. Named variables are created with the following syntax:

```
varname=varvalue
```

When this variable is used, it will be referred to as **$varname**. The dollar sign signifies that the word following is the variable's *name*. The variable's *value* will be substituted in its place. For example, suppose you define a variable as follows:

```
$ CHAMPIONS=Pistons
```

You can display the value of the variable with the following command:

```
$ echo $CHAMPIONS
```

The computer will respond by displaying:

```
Pistons
```

The variable name (to the left of the equals sign) must not contain any spaces. By convention, variable names are written in uppercase letters, but this is not required. The text string that constitutes the value of a variable (to the right of the equals sign) may contain spaces, but if it does, the string must be enclosed in double quotes. An example would be the following:

```
$ CHAMPIONS="Detroit Pistons"
$ echo $CHAMPIONS
Detroit Pistons
```

You can add $CHAMPIONS to the environment by exporting it with the following command:

```
$ export CHAMPIONS
```

The system assigns a number of environment variables to you, whether you define any or not. To see what environment variables are available, issue the **env** command. It displays a complete list of variables with their definitions. A typical display would be:

```
$ env
CHAMPIONS="Detroit Pistons"
DOSPATH=/usr/vpix/dosbin:.
HOME=/usr/allen
HZ=100
LOGNAME=allen
MAIL=/usr/mail/allen
PATH=:/bin:/usr/bin:/usr/vpix/dosbin:.:/usr/allen/bin
TERM=AT386
TZ=EST5EDT
VPIXCNF=/usr/allen/vpix/vpix.cnf
```

The system also maintains variables other than those listed by the **env** command. These include any local variables you may have defined and certain others, called standard variables. You can display these variables, along with the environment variables, by issuing the **set** command with no arguments:

```
$ set
CHAMPIONS="Detroit Pistons"
DOSPATH=/usr/vpix/dosbin:.
HOME=/usr/allen
HZ=100
IFS=
LOGNAME=allen
MAIL=/usr/mail/allen
MAILCHECK=600
OPTIND=1
PATH=:/bin:/usr/bin:/usr/vpix/dosbin:.:/usr/allen/bin
PS1=$
PS2=
TERM=AT386
TZ=EST5EDT
VPIX=/usr/allen/vpix/vpix.cnf
```

The **$HOME** variable gives the "address" of your home directory. **$IFS** contains the internal field separators (the space, tab, and newline characters), which are present but invisible in the above display. The **$PATH** variable shows which directories are searched when you issue a command. The primary prompt string is **$PS1**; it tells you that the shell is waiting for you to enter a command. The secondary prompt string. is **$PS2**. If you see the **$PS2** prompt, the shell is waiting for you to enter the rest of an incomplete command. The **$TERM** variable tells the system what kind of terminal you have. This information is used by **vi** and other screen-oriented programs to control the screen display.

Conditional Structures

To be genuinely useful, a program must be able to make decisions. It must be able to examine the result of a command and choose between two or more courses of action. The course chosen will be conditional on the result of the command.

An elementary form of conditional structure looks at whether a command has been executed successfully. If so, an exit status of zero (0) is returned. A failure to complete the command will return a nonzero exit status. As a programmer, you can test the exit status of a command and choose a course of action depending on whether the exit status is zero or not. The built-in shell variable (**$?**) contains the exit status of the last command executed. If execution was successful, it will contain a zero. If there was a failure to execute the command, the nonzero value of the variable will indicate how the last command failed.

The && Conditional Operator

Within a program, you can specify an action dependent on the exit status of a given command. The **&&** conditional operator provides one method. If you place two command pipelines on the same line, separated by **&&,** the second pipeline will be executed only if the exit status of the last command in the first pipeline is zero. Otherwise, execution will proceed immediately to the next line, ignoring the pipeline after the **&&** conditional. The **&&** conditional operator provides a very limited form of program branching, since the alternate branch can execute only a single pipeline before rejoining the main line of the program.

The || Conditional Operator

The || conditional operator is the opposite of the **&&** conditional operator. When two command pipelines are placed on a line, separated by the || conditional operator, the second pipe line will be executed only if the exit status of the last command of the first pipeline is not zero.

For example, suppose you are not sure whether the file named **newfile** is in the current directory, named **/usr/allen/temp.** You know that **newfile** *is* in directory **/usr/allen.** If **newfile** is indeed in the **temp** directory, you want to display its contents on the screen. If **newfile** is not already in the **temp** directory, you want to copy it there, and then display it. The following example copies **newfile** to the **temp** directory and displays **newfile**:

```
$ cd /usr/allen/temp
$ cat newfile || cp /usr/allen/newfile /usr/allen/temp ; cat newfile
cat: cannot open newfile
This is the first line of the file named newfile.
This is the last line of the file named newfile.
$
```

You see that **newfile** did not already exist in the **temp** directory, because the command to the left of the || conditional returned a nonzero exit status. As a result, the commands to the right of the || were executed. The file was copied to the current directory, and from there it was displayed on the screen using the **cat** command.

Note that a semicolon (;) was used to separate the **cp** command from the **cat** command. The semicolon is an *unconditional command separator,* while the **&&** and the || are both *conditional command separators.*

The **if** *Conditional Operator*

The **&&** and || conditionals are not easily applied when there is a choice among several different courses of action. The Bourne shell has other constructs designed for these more complex situations. The most common is the **if** conditional operator. It can handle blocks made up of multiple command lines. The general format is:

```
if
      if block
then
      then block
elif
      first elif block
   .
   .
   .
elif
      nth elif block
else
      else block
fi
```

If the last command in the **if** block returns a zero exit status, then the commands in the **then** block are executed. If the last command in the **if** block returns a nonzero exit status, the entire **then** block is skipped. The **elif** (else if) blocks and the **else** block are optional. An **elif** block is actually an **if** construct nested into the original **if** construct. Multiple levels of nesting of **if** constructs are allowed. The **else** block is executed only if neither the **then** block nor any of the **elif** blocks is executed. The **fi** keyword (**if** spelled backward) signals the end of the **if** construct.

The **if** construct would be of limited use if it executed the **then** block only if the last command of the **if** block returned a zero exit status. You may often want to make a program branch based on the value of a variable rather than on whether a command was successfully completed. By combining the **if** command with the **test** command, you can create a powerful conditional branching facility.

The `test` *Command*

The **test** command evaluates an expression and returns an exit status of zero if the expression has a true value; otherwise it returns a nonzero exit status. If the expression is a file, **test** can test for its existence and for any one of over a dozen file attributes. File attributes include such characteristics as:

- Is it readable?

- Is it writable?

- Is it executable?

- Is it a regular file?

- Is it a directory?

An expression can also be a comparison of one string variable against another, or of one numeric variable against another. String variables can be compared for identity or nonidentity. Numeric variables can be compared for all logical relationships, including equals, not equals, greater than, greater than or equal to, less than, and less than or equal to.

The following example illustrates the use of the **test** command in conjunction with the **if** conditional operator:

```
$ VAR1=1
$ if test $VAR1 = 1
>     then echo one
>elif test $VAR1 = 2
>     then echo two
>else echo error
>fi
one
$
```

Since the expression in the **if** block is true ($VAR1 = 1), the **then** block is executed and "one" is echoed to the screen. Note also that the secondary prompt string (>) appears at the beginning of each line of the **if** construct after the first one until the construct is completed with the **fi** keyword. The secondary prompt string indicates that the shell is looking for more input to complete the current command, even though you have pressed [Enter].

If the expression in the **if** block were false, the result would be different, as illustrated in the following example:

```
$ VAR1=2
$ if test $VAR = 1
>     then echo one
>elif test $VAR1 = 2
>     then echo two
>else echo error
>fi
two
$
```

In this case, the **if** block does not test true, so the **elif** block is tested. Since this block does test true, the word "two" is echoed. If neither the **if** block nor any of the **elif** blocks tests true, the **else** block will be executed. The result is illustrated below:

```
$ VAR1=321
$ if test $VAR1 = 1
>     then echo one
>elif test $VAR1 = 2
>     then echo two
>else echo error
>fi
error
$
```

The case Conditional Operator

The **if-then-else** construct discussed above is useful for choosing between two different courses of action. If there are more than two choices, however, the addition of further **elif** clauses makes the construct unwieldy and hard to comprehend. Where there are more than two possible courses of action, the **case** construct is usually best. It is briefer and easier to grasp than an equivalent **if-then-elif-else** structure.

In the following example, a variable containing the name of an Apollo moon-mission crew member will display the number of the mission he flew on.

```
$ x=Armstrong
$ case $x in
> Anders|Borman|Lovell) echo "$x flew on Apollo 8.";;
> Cernan|Stafford|Young) echo "$x flew on Apollo 10.";;
> Aldrin|Armstrong|Collins) echo "$x flew on Apollo 11.";;
> Bean|Conrad|Gordon) echo "$x flew on Apollo 12.";;
> Haise|Lovell|Swigert) echo "$x flew on Apollo 13.";;
> Mitchell|Roosa|Shepard) echo "$x flew on Apollo 14.";;
> Irwin|Scott|Worden) echo "$x flew on Apollo 15.";;
> Duke|Mattingly|Young) echo "$x flew on Apollo 16.";;
> Cernan|Evans|Schmitt) echo "$x flew on Apollo 17.";;
> *> echo "$x did not go to the Moon.";;
> esac
Armstrong flew on Apollo 11.
$
```

Within a **case** construct, the vertical bar (|) serves as a logical OR symbol rather than as a pipe symbol. Thus, if the crew member held in variable **$x** is either Aldrin, Armstrong, or Collins, the message mentioning Apollo 11 will be echoed. Note also that the **case** construct will look only for the first match. If **$x=Lovell,** the above example will always return the message, "Lovell flew on Apollo 8." The fact that Lovell flew also on Apollo 13 will not be indicated.

Performing the same function using the **if** construct would entail much more work::

```
$ x=Armstrong
$ if test $x = Anders -o $x = Borman -o $x = Lovell
>     then echo "$x flew on Apollo 8."
> elif test $x = Cernan -o $x = Stafford -o $x = Young
>     then echo "$x flew on Apollo 10."
> elif test $x = Aldrin -o $x = Armstrong -o $x = Collins
>     then echo "$x flew on Apollo 11."
> elif test $x = Bean -o $x = Conrad -o $x = Gordon
      then echo "$x flew on Apollo 12."
> elif test $x = Haise -o $x = Lovell -o $x = Swigert
>     then echo "$x flew on Apollo 13."
> elif test $x = Mitchell -o $x = Roosa -o $x = Shepard
>     then echo "$x flew on Apollo 14."
> elif test $x = Irwin -o $x = Scott -o $x = Worden
>     then echo "$x flew on Apollo 15."
> elif test $x = Duke -o $x = Mattingly -o $x = Young
>     then echo "$x flew on Apollo 16."
> elif test $x = Cernan -o $x = Evans -o $x = Schmitt
>     then echo "$x flew on Apollo 17."
> else echo "$x did not go to the Moon."
> fi
Armstrong flew on Apollo 11.
```

The **-o** operator is the logical OR recognized by the **test** command. Similarly, the **-a** operator is the logical AND, and the **!** operator is the unary negation operator. The **test** command described earlier, supports a number of other options. If you need to use one of these options, then you cannot use the **case** command, but must use **if-test** instead. However, in all other cases, you are probably better off using the **case** construct. Where the **case** construct took only 12 lines of code in the example above, the **if-test** construct takes 20. Furthermore, the lines are shorter and easier to understand in the **case** construct.

Looping Structures

Some applications call for a block of commands to be executed repeatedly. One way to achieve this in many computer languages is with an unconditional branch command of some sort, such as the **goto** command. The Bourne shell does not support any such command, nor does the C shell. To perform such a function from the shell prompt or in a shell script, you must use one of the *looping* constructs. Looping constructs continue to execute the same block of code until a specified condition is met, at which point looping will cease and execution will take up after the last keyword of the loop.

The `while` *Conditional Loop Operator*

As its name implies, the **while** construct will continue to loop through the commands it encloses as long as the condition it tests remains true. The syntax is shown below:

```
while condition block
        do command block
done
```

The condition block is a series of commands. The exit status of the last command in the series is examined. If it is zero, the while condition is satisfied and another pass through the loop is taken. If it is nonzero, the loop is skipped and the command immediately following the **done** keyword is executed. In most cases, the condition block consists of only one command, usually the **test** command. Like the **if** operator, the **while** operator cannot make comparisons. Each may be combined with the **test** command to decide what to execute next.

The command block following the **do** keyword is a series of commands that perform the actual work of the **while** loop. They will be executed again and again as long as the loop condition remains true. The **done** keyword marks the end of the **while** construct.

As an example of the use of the **while** loop, test your system's speed in copying a file to the null device over ten trials. One way would be:

```
$ COUNT=1
$ while test $COUNT -lt 11
>     do cp /usr/vpix/vpix /dev/null
>     echo "Loop $COUNT occurred on `date`"
>     COUNT=`expr $COUNT + 1`
> done
Loop 1 occurred on Sun Jul 30 22:21:53 EDT 1989
Loop 2 occurred on Sun Jul 30 22:21:54 EDT 1989
Loop 3 occurred on Sun Jul 30 22:21:54 EDT 1989
Loop 4 occurred on Sun Jul 30 22:21:55 EDT 1989
Loop 5 occurred on Sun Jul 30 22:21:56 EDT 1989
Loop 6 occurred on Sun Jul 30 22:21:56 EDT 1989
Loop 7 occurred on Sun Jul 30 22:21:57 EDT 1989
Loop 8 occurred on Sun Jul 30 22:21:57 EDT 1989
Loop 9 occurred on Sun Jul 30 22:21:58 EDT 1989
Loop 10 occurred on Sun Jul 30 22:21:58 EDT 1989
```

The **expr** command lets you treat the text variable **$COUNT** as if it were a numeric variable, so that you can increment it. The file **vpix,** which contains 219,856 bytes, can be copied to the null device, and a loop messages can be displayed at a rate of about two per second. If you run this routine when your hard disk is new and unfragmented, you will have a benchmark that you can use later. When you suspect your hard disk retrievals are slowing down, copy this benchmark file to a scratch directory and run the **while** loop again. If the loop shows a significant slowdown, it is time to clean up your fragmented disk by making a file-by-file backup, erasing all files on disk, then restoring from backup.

The until *Conditional Loop Operator*

The **until** loop construct works much like the **while** loop construct, except that it continues to loop only until the loop condition becomes true. In other words, it continues as long as the loop condition is false. You could write the benchmark loop described in the preceding section with the **until** construct just as easily as with the **while** construct.

```
$ COUNT=1
$ until test $COUNT -ge 11
>     do cp /usr/vpix/vpix /dev/null
>     echo "Loop $COUNT occurred on `date`"
>     COUNT=`expr $COUNT + 1`
> done
```

The result is similar to that shown in the preceding example, with the file copy and the display of the loop count taking about half a second.

The break Statement

The **break** statement lets you exit a loop and continue processing before the loop condition is satisfied. It is particularly useful for breaking out of infinite loops, in which the loop condition can never be satisfied. For example:

```
$ while true
> do
>     sleep 5
>     if cat newfile
>     then break
>     fi
> done
```

The sole function of the **true** command is to return a zero exit status. Since the exit status of the **true** command is always zero, any **while** loop that has **true** as its condition will continue to loop forever. In this example, the system waits five seconds, then tries to display the contents of a file named **newfile.** If **newfile** does not exist, a nonzero exit status is returned and the **then** clause is skipped. The **while** loop is executed repeatedly until a file named **newfile** is created by another process that is operating concurrently. As soon as **newfile** appears in the current directory, the **cat** command displays its contents, and the **break** command drops you out of the **while** loop. This example shows how one active process can affect another.

The continue Statement

The **continue** statement is weaker than the **break** statement. When a **break** statement within a looping construct is executed, the loop is exited immediately and execution proceeds to the next command after the loop. When a **continue** statement within a looping construct is executed, the rest of the commands in the current iteration of the loop are skipped. Execution proceeds once again from the top of the loop. So the **break** command breaks out of the loop entirely. The **continue** command continues looping after skipping the remaining commands in the current iteration of the loop.

The for Statement

Like the **while** and **until** operators, **for** is a looping construct. The syntax is:

```
for variable in arg1 arg2 arg3 ... argn
do
        command list
done
```

The number of arguments in the **in** clause determines the number of times the loop is executed. The first time through the loop, the variable is given the value of the first argument. The variable may then be used within the command list. On each succeeding iteration of the loop, the variable is assigned the value of the next argument.

This structure could be used, for example, to back up files in the current directory.

```
$ for FILE in chap1 chap2 chap3 chap4 chap5 chap6
>    do
>         cp $FILE /usr/backup
>    done
```

If you have named your files consistently, you could save time by using a wildcard, as illustrated in the following:

```
$ for FILE in chap*
>    do
>         cp $FILE /usr/backup
>    done
```

In this case, all chapter files will be copied to the **backup** directory on your hard disk.

Although the **for** statement is often used to manipulate files, its arguments need not represent files. They can be any text string, as follows:

```
$ for STRING in 10 9 8 7 6 5 4 3 2 1
>    do
>         echo Execution suspended for $STRING more seconds.
>         sleep 1
>    done
```

This command causes a 10-second delay in execution, displaying the amount of delay remaining in the form of a 10-second countdown.

The expr Command

Use the **expr** command to evaluate expressions. Although it can be used with text expressions, **expr** is most valuable in evaluating numeric expressions of the following form:

```
expression operator expression
```

The operator is one of the following binary operators:

```
*    multiplication
/    division
%    remainder
+    addition
-    subtraction
```

144

The order in which they are listed is the order of their precedence. The **expr** command will evaluate all multiplications in an expression before it looks at any additions. Operations can be grouped with parentheses where the normal order of precedence would yield an incorrect result.

Parentheses, the asterisk, and the slash have special meanings to the shell. Since the shell examines all arguments of a command before surrendering control to the command, it will see these special characters in an **expr** command and take the wrong action before the **expr** command is given a chance to execute. To prevent this, you must escape each special character in an expression by preceding it with a backslash (\). The backslash tells the shell to ignore any special meaning of the immediately following character.

A simple use of the **expr** command would be:

```
$ expr 3 + 11
14
$
```

A more complex example using escaped characters would be:

```
$ expr \( 3 \* 4 + 2 \) \/ 2
7
$
```

Note that a space is mandatory between each number and operator. The **expr** command uses blanks as delimiters between operands.

The exit Command

The **exit** command can be used to terminate a Unix session and log out the user. The **exit** command has a different function when executed within a shell script; it immediately aborts the script and returns control to the shell prompt.

When used within a shell script, the **exit** command takes a single optional argument. When the **exit** command is executed, its argument (if any) is returned to the shell. You can use this fact to determine which of several possible paths through a script was actually taken. For example, you might have a structure such as the following:

```
$ VARIABLE=value3
$ case $VARIABLE in
>     value1)
>         command list 1
>         exit 1 ;;
>     value2)
>         command list 2
>         exit 2 ;;
>     value3)
>         command list 3
>         exit 3 ;;
>     *)
>         exit 0 ;;
> esac
$ EXITSTAT = $?
$ echo $EXITSTAT
3
```

To remain consistent with Unix's convention, return a zero value if execution was successful. If execution was unsuccessful, return a nonzero value that will give a clue to the nature of the failure.

Comparing Files

The shell has two commands for comparing files to see whether they are identical. The first, **cmp,** works with all kinds of files, including binary files. The second, **diff**, works only with text files, but outputs information that is much more helpful than that displayed by **cmp.** The Unix shell's **cmp** command gives you only about as much information as does the DOS **comp** command, which performs a similar function.

The output of the **cmp** command is illustrated in the following example. First, create a file using the **vi** text editor:

```
$ vi testfile1
Continuing education becomes increasingly important as advances
in technology change the complexion of the workplace.  In order
to remain competitive, companies in all fields must employ
people who are up to date on the latest developments in their
field as will as on advances in management theory.
~
~
~
"testfile1" 5 lines, 301 characters
```

Next, create a file that is slightly different. In the second file, correct the spelling error in the fifth line (*will* should be *well*).

```
$ vi testfile2
Continuing education becomes increasingly important as advances
in technology change the complexion of the workplace.  In order
to remain competitive, companies in all fields must employ
people who are up to date on the latest developments in their
field as well as on advances in management theory.
~
~
~
"testfile2" 5 lines, 301 characters
```

Now compare the two files using the **cmp** command:

```
$ cmp testfile1 testfile2
testfile1 testfile2 differ: char 261, line 5
$
```

This terse display tells you that the two files differ and gives the character number and the line number where the difference occurs.

The **diff** command shows the differences between the two files much more clearly. Using the same two test files, the display would be:

```
$ diff testfile1 testfile2
5c5
< field as will as on advances in management theory.
---
> field as well as on advances in management theory.
$
```

The display indicates that line 5 of the first file is changed in line 5 of the second file (5c5). The appropriate line from file 1 is displayed, followed by the corresponding line from file 2. Only a quick glance is needed to spot the difference. Several options are available with **diff,** one of which lets you use the **diff** command with the **ed** editor to make the second file identical to the first.

Finding a Text String in a File

The DOS **find** command is used to search for a specified text string in a file or group of files. The Unix **find** command, however, has a completely different function. The Unix shell command that is used to search for a text string is **grep,** with its variants **fgrep** and **egrep.** Specify a text string and a file or group of files to the **grep** command. The text string may be specified directly, or with a regular expression. The **grep** command will find all occurrences of the string and display the lines in which they occur.

A number of options allow you to customize the search. For example, the **-v** option selects every line in the specified file(s) that does *not* contain the search string. The **-c** option tells only how many lines contain the search string. The **-n** option displays the lines containing the search string along with their line numbers.

The **fgrep** command will not accept a regular expression as input. You must specify the search string as a fixed string only. However, **fgrep** conducts its search considerably faster than does **grep.**

Like **grep, egrep** accepts regular expressions, and also provides some operations not available with **grep.** The tradeoff is a longer search time.

Any of the three **grep** commands could have been used with equal success in the following example:

```
$ fgrep -n on testfile2
1:Continuing education becomes increasingly important as advances
2:in technology change the complexion of the workplace. In order
4:people who are up to date on the latest developments in their
5:field as well as on advances in management theory.
$
```

Every line containing the text string "on" is displayed, including those where the two letters happen to appear together within a word. To locate only the word "on," the specification would have been:

```
$ fgrep -n " on " testfile2
4:people who are up to date on the latest developments in their
5:field as well as on advances in management theory.
$
```

In this case, the blanks on both sides of the word "on" guarantee that only lines containing the word will be retrieved.

Sorting the Contents of Files

The Unix **sort** command can do everything the DOS **sort** command does, and more. The Unix command offers several options that are not available with the corresponding DOS command, including the ability to sort several source files simultaneously and merge them into a single destination file. By default, the Unix **sort** is case-sensitive, meaning that a line with a sort key of **Zetetics** will come before a line with a sort key of **anthropology.**

Sort assumes that a file is made up of a number of lines, with each line consisting of one or more fields. You can specify one of those fields as the primary sort key, and a second as a secondary sort key. There may be any number of sort keys, but later sort keys only have an effect if all earlier sort keys are identical for a particular line. If you do not specify a sort key, the file will be sorted in ascending order, starting with the first character of each line.

The **-u** (unique) option, will display only one instance of each sort key, regardless of how many times that key appears. This is a good way to remove redundant lines while merging two files that have a significant amount of information in common. Suppose you had one file containing the names of several New Jersey cities:

```
$ cat njcities
Nutley
Belleville
Newark
Wildwood
$
```

In another file were the names of some Ohio cities:

```
$ cat ohcities
Hiram
Aurora
Newark
Urbana
Ada
$
```

Sorting them with the **-u** option will sort each file, merge them, then remove any duplicate city names. The syntax is:

```
$ sort -u njcities ohcities
```

The resulting display is:

```
Ada
Aurora
Belleville
Hiram
Newark
Nutley
Urbana
Wildwood
$
```

The lists have been sorted and merged, and the duplicate "Newark" has been removed.

Removing Redundant Lines from Files

The **uniq** command is a more general tool for dealing with a sorted file that contains duplicate lines or records. When used without options, it works like the **-u** option of the **sort** command, removing all redundant lines. The **-u** option of the **uniq** command outputs only those lines that were already unique in the input file. The **-d** option outputs only those lines that were duplicated in the input file. The **-c** option, like the default option, displays one copy of each line, regardless of how many times it appeared in the input file. The difference between the **-c** option and the default is that the **-c** option also displays the number of copies of each line that existed in the input file, as shown in the following example:

```
$ sort njcities ohcities > cities
$ cat cities
Ada
Aurora
Belleville
Hiram
Newark
Newark
Nutley
Urbana
Wildwood
$ uniq -c cities
1 Ada
1 Aurora
1 Belleville
1 Hiram
2 Newark
1 Nutley
1 Urbana
1 Wildwood
```

"Newark" is listed only once, but the number preceding it shows that there were two copies of "Newark" in the input file.

Moving Data between Files

Unix System V provides you with a means to move data using the **cut** and **paste** commands. Xenix does not have the **cut** and **paste** commands, so this subsection does not apply to Xenix.

The **cut** and **paste** commands make certain assumptions about the format of the data in files. They assume that each line of the file represents a distinct record, and that each record is composed of one or more fields. The fields are separated by a delimiter character, the default delimiter being [Tab]. You can specify an alternate delimiter if you wish. Any legal character may be used.

The **cut** command is best explained with an example. Consider the following file, named **snip:**

```
Westminster:Orange
Rosemead:Los Angeles
Escondido:San Diego
Barstow:San Bernardino
Palm Springs:Riverside
```

The first field is the name of a Southern California city; the second is the name of the county within which the city is located. The colon (:) is the delimiter that separates the two fields.

The following example cuts out the counties, leaving only the cities, and sends the result to a new file named **cities.**

```
$ cut -f1 -d: snip > cities
$ cat cities
Westminster
Rosemead
Escondido
Barstow
Palm Springs
$
```

The first argument of the **cut** command, **-f1**, specifies that field 1 be retained. All other fields are cut out. The second argument, **-d:**, specifies that the field delimiter is the colon. Since the colon is the delimiter, **cut** properly handles multiword fields such as Palm Springs without the need for quotes.

Another file containing only the county names can be created in a similar manner.

```
$ cut -f2 -d: snip > counties
$ cat counties
Orange
Los Angeles
San Diego
San Bernardino
Riverside
$
```

With the **cut** command, you can specify exactly the fields you want.

Once you have used the **cut** command to extract desired fields from one or more existing files, you can use the **paste** command to reassemble them in a new way. To illustrate the principle, paste the cities and counties back together, but this time with the counties listed first. You would use the following command:

```
$ paste -d: counties cities  newsnip
$ cat newsnip
Orange:Westminster
Los Angeles:Rosemead
San Diego:Escondido
San Bernardino:Barstow
Riverside:Palm Springs
```

Once again, the colon has been specified as the delimiter, separating the county names from the city names.

Suspending Execution for a Specified Time Period

In a multitasking system, you may not want *every* process you initiate to execute immediately. It makes sense to run some lower-priority tasks when the system is lightly loaded, perhaps at night. You probably don't want to return to the office in the middle of the night, just to start a low-priority job, so Unix gives you the capability to launch a job but delay its execution until later. This is accomplished with the **sleep** command.

The **sleep** command causes a delay equal to the number of seconds you specify in its argument. For example, the command **sleep 3600** will cause a delay of one hour before returning control to the shell. By using the sleep command in a shell script, you can delay a large job until a time when you know system activity will be low.

Searching the Directory Tree for Files

The **find** command is one of the most complex and powerful in the Unix repertoire. It has no parallel in DOS. This command searches through specified directories, selecting files that meet criteria specified in the command line.

Although the **find** command has many possible uses, probably the most common is to locate a file when you have forgotten what directory it is in. If your disk is cluttered with multiple copies of the same file, you can use **find** to ferret them out. In the following simple example, the system searches for all occurrences of the file **RISCchips** in the current directory and its subdirectories:

```
$ find . -name RISCchips -print
./temp/RISCchips
./RISCbook/resources/RISCchips
./RISCbook/RISCchips
$
```

The period (.) denotes the current directory. The second argument, **-name**, tells you that the following argument is the name of the file for which you are searching. The last argument, **-print**, causes the result to be printed to standard output. Without the **-print** argument, the **find** command would not show you any results.

You can use wildcards to retrieve a group of files with similar names. In the following example, all files in the **/usr** directory and its subdirectories are checked; any file name that starts with the letter *x* and ends with a decimal digit will be retrieved:

```
$ find /usr -name "x*[0-9]" -print
/usr/lib/tabset/xerox1720
/usr/include/X11/bitmaps/xlogo16
/usr/include/X11/bitmaps/xlogo32
/usr/include/X11/bitmaps/xlogo64
$
```

Sometimes files can grow to be very large without your noticing. Files that keep a log of commands or errors are an example. As your disk fills up, performance suffers. You can use the **find** command to check for the presence of unusually large files:

```
$ find / -size +500 -print
/xenix
/usr/lib/sysadm/sysadm.menu
/usr/lib/X11/fonts/k14.snf
/usr/sys/conf/xenix
/usr/sys/conf/xenix-
/usr/xbin/standalone/Xsight
/usr/xbin/standalone/mwm
/xenix.old
$
```

This command causes the system to search the root directory and all its subdirectories (that is, the entire file system) for any files that are larger than 500 blocks (each block is 512 bytes). In this example, several files associated with the Xenix operating system itself are that large, as are several files associated with the X11 Window System. There appear to be no other overly large files, so this system does not yet have a problem with log files that have run amok.

The third argument in the example, **+500**, specified a file size of greater than 500 blocks. An argument of **-500** would specify files less than 500 blocks. (There will be a lot of these.) An argument of **500** would specify files that are exactly 500 blocks in length.

Another important use of the **find** command is locating files according to when they were last modified. The **-mtime** argument says that the next argument specifies the number of days to search for file-change activity. In the following example, the **find** command retrieves all files (including directory files) in the current directory and its subdirectories that have been changed within the last two days:

```
$ find . -mtime -2 -print
.
./temp
./temp/RISCchips
./snip
./RISCbook
./RISCbook/resources
./RISCbook/resources/RISCchips
./RISCbook/RISCchips
$
```

The following **find** command retrieves all files in the current directory and its subdirectories that were last changed two or more days ago:

```
$ find . -mtime +2 -print
./.profile
./chap1
./chap2
./chap3
./chap4
./chap5
./chap6
./testfile1
./testfile2
./temp/chap1
./temp/demo
./temp/newfile
./newfile
./demo
$
```

There are many more **find** command options than those mentioned in the preceding examples, which are employed by Unix experts in a wide variety of situations. As you become more proficient in shell programming, you will use the **find** command more and more.

Creating Shell Scripts

Shell commands are very useful when executed from the shell prompt, as shown in the preceding examples. They are even more valuable when put together into a shell script. The shell commands available with Unix are comprehensive enough to form a respectable programming language. It is even possible to write an application as a shell script, although this would be unusual. Shell scripts do not execute as fast as compiled applications, since they must be handled by a shell interpreter rather than executed directly by the Unix kernel.

Shell scripts are ideal for utilities and for fairly complex operations that must be performed frequently. A shell script is executed by a *subshell*, which may be invoked explicitly or implicitly. Build a shell script using a text editor such as **vi** or **ed.** The following simple example was created with **vi**.

```
$ cat command.file
pwd
ls -l c*
$
```

The script displays the name of the current directory, then gives a detailed directory listing of all files that begin with the letter *c*. When you create a file in this way, execute permission is not granted to anyone. You can get around this problem by explicitly invoking a subshell as shown in the following example:

```
$ sh command.file
/usr/allen
-rw-r--r--   1 allen     group      67 Aug  6 23:48 cities
-rw-r--r--   1 allen     group      14 Aug 10 23:01 command.file
$
```

As you can see, the command file was executed, even though execute permission is absent from the permissions block at the head of its directory listing.

It is also possible to execute a shell script without explicitly calling a subshell, but you must first change the permission on the script file to allow execution:

```
$ chmod u+x command.file
$ command.file
/usr/allen
-rw-r--r--   1 allen     group      67 Aug  6 23:48 cities
-rwxr--r--   1 allen     group      14 Aug 10 23:01 command.file
$
```

The result is the same as with the **sh** command, except that the user now has execute (x) permission for **command.file.**

You may include shell scripts as commands within other scripts. Such *subscripts* behave exactly as if they were invoked from the shell prompt. Remember, however, that variables defined in the parent script will not be carried down to the subscript unless they are exported with the **expr** command.

Within a shell script, the pound sign (#) indicates that what follows is a comment, a note on the purpose and operation of the script. When the shell interpreter sees a pound sign, it ignores everything beyond the sign up to the end of the line. Shell comments do not slow performance, so they may be used liberally.

Using Replaceable Parameters

When you write a shell script, you may not have all the information that the script will need when it is executed. You can pass this information to the script at run time using *replaceable parameters*. Replaceable parameters are variables that serve as shell-script arguments. When the script is executed, these variables are replaced with the actual values. For example, the following simple script displays the current directory, changes to a new directory whose name is entered at run time by the operator, then displays the directory again:

```
$ cat parameter
pwd    # Display directory name
cd $1 # Change to directory named by operator
pwd    # Display new directory name
$ sh parameter temp
/usr/allen
/usr/allen/temp
$ pwd
/usr/allen
$
```

The change of directory is only effective within the script. Once the script is complete, the current directory reverts to what it was before the script was entered, as the result of the final **pwd** command shows.

The Login Shell Script

While the AUTOEXEC.BAT batch file sets up the operating environment of a DOS system, the Unix environment is configured by a shell script. In a DOS system, AUTOEXEC.BAT is run every time the computer is powered up or reset. Since Unix is a multiuser system, setup takes place every time a user logs in. There are two login scripts.

The first login script is named **profile** and contains system defaults that are the same for all users. It is maintained by the system administrator and may not be modified by individual users. In most systems, it resides in the **/etc** directory. The Xenix 2.3

version of **/etc/profile** contains only comments when installed. The system administrator can add commands that are appropriate for this particular installation and that are common to all users.

In contrast, the **profile** delivered with Interactive's Unix System V/386 Release 3.2 is quite extensive:

```
#ident  "@(#)profile    2.6 - 98/03/15"
#The profile that all logins get before using their own .profile

trap "" 1 2 3
umask 022          # set default file creation mask
. /etc/TIMEZONE

case "$0" in
-sh | -rsh)
# calculate available disk space in root filesystem.
    echo ""        # skip a line
    . /etc/dfspace

# issue message of the day
    trap : 1 2 3
    echo ""          # skip a line
    if [ -s /etc/motd ] ; then cat /etc/motd; fi
    trap ""  2 3
# set default attributes for terminal
    stty erase '^h' echoe

    if [ x$TERM = x -o "$TERM" = "unknown" ]; then
        LOGTTY=${LOGTTY:=`tty`}
        TERM=AT386             # default terminal type
    fi
    export TERM

# check mailbox and news bulletins
    if mail -e
    then echo "you have mail"
    fi
    if [ $LOGNAME != root ]
    then news -n
    fi
    ;;
-su)
    :
    ;;
esac
export PATH;
trap 1 2 3
```

As this script shows, **profile** handles such housekeeping chores as calculating the amount of disk space available, displaying the message of the day, setting the default attributes of the terminal, and checking for mail and news bulletins. You can learn a lot about how shell scripts work by studying the **profile** on your system.

Immediately after **/etc/profile** is completed, the second login script, located in the user's home directory, is run. This second script, named **.profile**, may be customized to reflect the user's preferences, since each user has one. You may use your **.profile** script to override defaults set by **/etc/profile**, to initialize variables, or even to switch from the Bourne shell to an alternate one such as C or Korn. The **.profile** script specifies such items as the directory where your mail will be stored, new directories to be added to the standard PATH, and variables that apply to applications you have installed.

Different **.profile** scripts may vary greatly, depending on the version of Unix and on the preferences of the individual user. However, they all have the same purpose: to make the operating environment more comfortable and convenient to the user.

The Dot (.) Command

The **.profile** file is normally executed when you log in. You may change the script at any time with your favorite text editor. In order to make your changes effective, you must execute the script. This process can be more complicated than it seems. One foolproof way of making sure that your modified environment goes into effect is to log out, then log in again. The act of logging in will automatically execute your new **.profile** script. Because modifying your environment is a five step process (invoke the editor, make the change, log out, log in, and test the change), it can become tedious if you are debugging a major change. You may need to repeat the process many times.

An alternative would be to execute the **.profile** script directly after modifying it. You might think the appropriate syntax would be:

```
$ sh .profile
```

Although this syntax would work well for just about any other shell script, it will not work with **.profile**. Remember that when you run a shell script, a subshell is created to perform the execution. Remember also that variables declared in a subshell are not automatically transferred up to the parent shell. Thus, after you exit the script and return to your original shell, any changes to variables that you may have made in the script will not be reflected in your operating environment, unless you exported the variables after declaring them.

The dot command lets you avoid this problem. It directs the current shell to execute the command that follows it on the command line rather than spawning a subshell to do it. Syntax is as follows:

```
$ . .profile
```

Errors and Error Messages

If your shell script contains an error, Unix will "protest" when it attempts to execute the script, displaying a brief error message before returning control to the user. If you are executing the script with the **sh** command, two options can help you find the problem. The verbose option, called for by the **-v** flag, displays the script commands as they are executing, thus giving you a context within which to evaluate the error message when it appears. The trace option does the same but also substitutes the values of variables for the names of variable in the display. The trace option also displays a plus sign (+) as the first character of all commands except variable assignment commands. Use the verbose and trace options when debugging a new and unproven shell script. You will be able to perfect it much more quickly.

THE C SHELL

The C shell was originally developed for use with the Berkeley versions of Unix. It is a command interpreter like the Bourne shell, but with several important differences. The C shell has been optimized to be used interactively from a terminal. The Bourne shell is better suited for executing shell scripts. Choose a shell based on the needs of your particular task.

Most of the foregoing discussion of Bourne-shell syntax applies as well to the corresponding C-shell commands. This section will now discuss several features of the C shell that are lacking in the Bourne shell.

Command History

The C shell keeps a log of all commands entered. This log remains available for inspection and can be used to reexecute commands without having to reenter them. You can set a variable for the number of previous commands that the shell "remembers;" it can be as many as you wish. If this **history** variable is not set, the shell keeps only the immediately previous command. To set it to a larger value, use a command such as the following:

```
% set history=20
```

When this command executes, the shell begins logging every command entered and will retain the twenty most recent ones. This log can help you trace a sequence of events that led to an unexpected result.

The log also allows you to use an argument from a previous command in a new command. The **!** operator indicates that you are taking something from the history file. To take the argument from the immediately previous command, use **!$**, as demonstrated by the following:

```
% ls -l cities
-rw-r--r--   1 allen     other        52 Aug  7 23:03 cities
% cat !$
cat cities
Westminster
Rosemead
Escondido
Barstow
Palm Springs
%
```

In this example, when the shell recognizes the **!$** operator, it goes back to the previous command (**ls**) and combines its argument with the current command (**cat**) to create the desired effect. The new command is echoed to the screen (**cat cities**) before it is executed, which in this example, causes the city names to be listed. Because this example is fairly simple, you don't save much time by using the history file. However, if a command argument is large and complex, using the **!$** operator may save you time.

Reexecuting long commands you have used earlier saves keystrokes. To reexecute a command, first display the history log by issuing the **history** command, then retrieve the command by referring to the number that the history log automatically assigned it. Issue the **history** command as follows:

```
% history
    35   set history=20
    36   ls -l cities
    37   cat cities
    38   history
%
```

The most recent entry in the log will be the **history** command itself. To reexecute a command in the log, retrieve it by number. The following example tells the shell to retrieve command number 36, display it, then executed it:

```
% !36
ls -l cities
-rw-r--r--   1 allen    other        52 Aug  7 23:03 cities
%
```

The same result can be obtained with the **!l** command. This syntax tells the shell to look for the most recent command that starts with the letter *l*, then display and execute it. This variation of the **!** command is handy when you remember the first character of the command you want, therefore, you need not display the log to find its number.

You can perform limited editing of a command retrieved from the history log with the caret (^) operator. Consider the following:

```
% cat cities
Westminster
Rosemead
Escondido
Barstow
Palm Springs
% ^cat^echo
echo cities
cities
%
```

The caret command is used in pairs, and operates on the immediately previous command. The string from the previous command, which appears after the first caret, is replaced by the string after the second caret. This modified command is displayed, then executed. In the example above, the string *cat* is replaced by the string *echo*. This creates a new command (**echo cities**).

Aliases

The **alias** command allows you to use a shortened or easily remembered alternate name for a Unix command. For example, if you are accustomed to DOS syntax and commands, you can create an alias that allows you to use these familiar commands instead of the Unix ones. The following example illustrates how you would assign the alias **dir** for the **ls -l** command:

```
% alias dir ls -l
```

Now, whenever you enter the command **dir,** you will get the same display that you would see if you had entered **ls -l.**

You can put your alias definitions into a file named **.cshrc**, which will be read every time you log into the C shell, thus automatically putting your aliases into effect. Custom default aliases maintained in the **.cshrc** file can be handy, but do not overuse this feature. Performance could be unfavorably affected, since the system must read the aliases and put them into effect every time you log in. Don't keep more than 10 to 15 aliases in your **.cshrc file.**

SHELL PROGRAMS VS. COMPILED PROGRAMS

Shell scripts can be alternatives to writing programs in regular programming languages such as C or Pascal. There are pros and cons to this use of shell scripts. On the positive side, you can develop a shell script more quickly than an equivalent program in a compiled language. Since the shell interprets scripts directly, you do not need to recompile every time you make a change to a script you are developing. On the other hand, a script executes more slowly than an equivalent compiled program. The interpreter must parse the script commands every time the script is executed. Thus for a complicated application that will be run only a few times, writing a shell script may be a better choice. If you are writing an application that will be used many times and for which performance is an important consideration, a shell script may not be appropriate.

The shell command language has strong capabilities for manipulating text and files. If the task before you involves text or files, give serious consideration to writing a shell script to accomplish it. If the task involves operating on numeric data, a shell script is probably not a good choice.

MULTIPROCESSING

Shells may be nested, meaning you can start a subshell from your currently running shell. In fact, you can run multiple subprocesses at once, using the *shell-layer manager*, which is invoked with the **shl** command. The shell layer manager lets you create as many as seven subshells, called layers. Only the current layer accepts input from the keyboard, but programs in all layers may be executing simultaneously. Programs executing in any layer may send output to the terminal screen.

You could, for example, create a document in one layer, using **vi,** while toggling occasionally to another layer to retrieve information to be included in the document. The dialogue to initiate this *multiprocessing* would be similar to the following:

```
$ shl
>>> create
(1) vi thesis
```

When the **shl** command is executed, the **>>>** prompt is displayed as an alert to you that the shell-layer manager is now in control, and only shell-layer manager commands will be accepted. The **create** command creates a new layer, then starts it running. **(1)** is the prompt for the first layer. The **vi thesis** command starts the **vi** editor and opens a document named **thesis.** After you have finished entering text, return to the shell-layer editor by pressing [Ctrl-z]. The shell-layer prompt appears, allowing you to create a second layer. In this new layer, you can perform operations to get information relevant to the document being created in layer 1. At any time, you can leave layer 2 by pressing [Ctrl-z]. Once you are back at the shell-layer manager prompt, use either the **resume 1** or the **toggle** command to reenter the first layer exactly where you left it.

SUMMARY

The shell is not an integral part of Unix, but is in fact an application program. The Unix shell environment is similar to the DOS batch environment, but much more comprehensive and flexible. A variety of shells is available, and you are free to write your own. The most commonly used is the Bourne shell.

The most important features of the C shell distinguishing it from the Bourne shell are command history and aliasing. The C shell is optimized for interactive use from the terminal. If you need primarily to execute scripts, with little terminal interaction, the Bourne shell is probably more appropriate for you.

The shell-layer manager is the mechanism that allows a user at a single terminal to control as many as seven simultaneously executing tasks. This capability is different from background processing. Background processing permits the user to set a task in motion, but the user may not interact with it again except to kill it.

Chapter 13

System Administration

I n a DOS system, system administration is not a very big job. Since DOS is a single-user system, each user performs the system administration tasks for his or her own system. These tasks consist mostly of setting the system time and date, backing up the hard disk periodically, and cleaning out obsolete files when the disk becomes too full.

A multiuser system such as Unix requires more attention from the system administrator. The overall job of the system administrator is to maintain the integrity of the system. To perform that function effectively, he or she must have broad powers to change the system hardware and the file systems that reside on it. These powers are granted to only one person, the superuser.

THE SUPERUSER

The person who logs in with a login name of **root** is called the superuser. The superuser can bypass all the security provisions of a Unix system in order to efficiently maintain system integrity. Among the tasks involved are installing new software, adapting software to the local system, performing periodic backups, recovering lost data, maintaining security, and changing the system configuration.

To perform such tasks, the superuser must have the power to change just about any aspect of the system. If no one had such power, users would find that small problems suddenly became major ones. For example, suppose someone left your company without telling anyone his or her password. The superuser can access the ex-user's files and reassign them to a colleague before removing the ex-user's login ID. Important files are preserved for the benefit of the organization, and the former user will no longer be able to log in.

Of course, the broad powers afforded to the superuser carry with them a concomitant danger. An inexperienced superuser could inadvertently cause considerable damage. Even worse, a malicious superuser could wipe out the entire system.

Ideally, only one person, the system administrator, should know the superuser password. Sometimes, however, a person may be incapacitated or unavailable, and a backup must be ready. In any case, only a very few highly trusted and knowledgeable people should be in a position to exercise superuser privileges.

Even such trusted users should use the **root** login only for tasks that cannot be accomplished any other way. To perform their normal work, they should log out as superuser and log in again under their own personal login name. That reduces the danger of inadvertently performing an action that affects other users' files adversely. If they make such a mistake while logged in under their own name, the system may complain but will not perform the restricted action. However, if they are logged in as superuser, the system will go right ahead and damage another user's files.

Logging in as root

There are two ways for a person who knows the superuser password to gain superuser privileges. The most straightforward is to log in as **root**, then enter the superuser password. The system will respond by displaying the superuser PS1 (prompt), which is the pound sign (#). The superuser PS1 is different from the normal user's PS1 ($), to constantly remind you that you are logged in as superuser and should exercise caution.

When you log in as **root**, your home directory is the **root** directory of the file system (/). Your default search path is also different from that of a normal user. Your own personal home directory is not included. The system recognizes you only as the superuser. Because, as superuser, you should be mainly concerned with system administration, your path includes the directories where system administration commands are stored. To access someone's personal files, you will have to specify the path to them.

The su Command

A second way to gain superuser privileges is to issue the **su** command. When you execute the **su** command from your user shell, a subshell is created that temporarily gives you the identity of the superuser or some other user. If you issue the **su** command with no argument, Unix will assume that you want to temporarily assume the identity of the superuser, and will ask you for the superuser password. If you issue the **su** command with some other user's login name as an argument, Unix assumes you want to temporarily assume the identity of that other user, and it will ask you for the user's password. If you enter the password correctly, you will gain the privileges of the superuser or of the other user you specified. When you are finished, enter the **exit** command to terminate the subshell and return to your original login shell.

Becoming the superuser by using the **su** command is not the same as logging in as superuser. When you use the **su** command, your home directory remains the same, rather than changing to the system **root** directory. To change your home directory to the system **root** directory (or to the home directory of the target user), use the minus (−) argument with **su**, as shown in the following example:

```
$ su
# pwd
/usr/allen
# exit
$ su -
# pwd
/
#
```

SYSTEM ADMINISTRATION SHELLS

Recently, the advent of system administration shells has made the most commonly performed system administration tasks a good deal easier to perform. These menu-driven visual shells lead the system administrator through a step-by-step procedure for each task.

The exact form of the shell will vary from one version of Unix to another, as will the command to invoke it. For example, in SCO Xenix, the superuser may invoke the shell by typing **sysadmsh**. A bar menu will appear, displaying the various functional choices. With Interactive Unix V/386 Release 3.2, the shell is invoked by typing **sysadm**. The following menu is displayed:

```
        SYSTEM ADMINISTRATION

   1 diskmgmt        disk management menu
   2 filemgmt        file management menu
   3 machinemgmt     machine management menu
   4 packagemgmt     package management menu
   5 softwaremgmt    software management menu
   6 syssetup        system setup menu
   7 ttymgmt         tty management menu
   8 usermgmt        user management menu

   Enter a number, a name, the initial part of a name, or
   ? or <number>? for HELP,  ^ to GO BACK,  q to QUIT:
```

If the appearance of your system administrator shell is different from what is shown in the preceding example, the functions will still be much the same. This chapter will examine each menu option in turn to gain an appreciation of the variety of tasks the system administrator is called upon to perform.

The Disk Management Menu

Proper management of the storage resources of a computer system is one of the system administrator's most important tasks. If you select **1** from the **sysadm** menu shown above, the following menu will appear:

```
DISK MANAGEMENT

1 checkfsys      check a removable medium file system for errors
2 cpdisk        make exact copies of a removable medium
3 erase         erase data from removable medium
4 format        format new removable diskettes
5 harddisk      hard disk management menu
6 makefsys      create a new file system on a removable medium
7 mountfsys     mount a removable medium file system
8 umountfsys    unmount a removable medium file system

Enter a number, a name, the initial part of a name, or
? or <number>? for HELP,  ^ to GO BACK,  q to QUIT:
```

All the options on the Disk Management menu deal with the management of removable media, except option **5,** which leads to a submenu covering hard-disk management. The Hard Disk Management menu is shown below:

```
HARD DISK MANAGEMENT

1 addbadblocks     enter bad sector information
2 addharddisk      add additional hard disk drives
3 checkhdfsys      check a hard disk file system for errors
4 display          display hard disk partitioning
5 mounthdfsys      mounts a hard disk file system
6 umounthdfsys     unmount a hard disk file system

Enter a number, a name, the initial part of a name, or
? or <number>? for HELP,  ^ to GO BACK,  q to QUIT:
```

If you suspect that your hard disk has problems, you can check for errors with option **3**. If you find errors, you can add them to the bad block table with option **1**. The operating system automatically maps around any bad blocks that are entered in the table, thus preventing them from affecting operations.

The File Management Menu

From the File Management menu, you can extract various facts about your files, such as how old they are, how large they are, and how much disk space they take up. Most important, however, are the options that deal with file backup and restoration. Information can be lost from files, more often than not through operator error. The importance of keeping copies of important files at a site remote from the computer cannot be overemphasized.

The File Management menu makes backup simple. Since the simplicity of a backup procedure is directly proportional to the likelihood that it will be faithfully carried out, the use of this menu could greatly improve your system integrity. The File Management menu is shown below:

```
                     FILE MANAGEMENT

  1 backup    backup files from built-in disk to removable disk
  2 busched   backup reminder scheduling menu
  3 diskuse   display how much of the built-in disks are being used
  4 fileage   list files older than a particular date
  5 filesize  list the largest files in a particular diretory
  6 restore   restore files from "backup" & "store" to built-in disk
  7 store     store files and file directories onto removable media

  Enter a number, a name, the initial part of a name, or
  ? or <number>? for HELP,  ^ to GO BACK,  q to QUIT:
```

The Machine Management Menu

The Machine Management menu has only one option. It tells you what users are logged in, what terminals they are on, and when they logged in. The Machine Management menu is shown below:

```
                   MACHINE MANAGEMENT

  1 whoson    print list of users currently logged onto the system

  Enter a number, a name, the initial part of a name, or
  ? or <number>? for HELP,  ^ to GO BACK,  q to QUIT:
```

The Package Management Menu

Like the operating system, some application packages need management attention from time to time. If these applications have been properly designed, their management operations can be integrated into the operating-system-management shell as selections on the Package Management menu. In the following example, two of the applications installed on the system have been designed to be administered from the **sysadm** system:

```
PACKAGE MANAGEMENT

1 pmgmt          print spooler management menu
2 vpixmgmt       VP/ix management menu

Enter a number, a name, the initial part of a name, or
? or <number>? for HELP,  ^ to GO BACK,  q to QUIT:
```

The print spooler manages the assignment of print jobs to the appropriate printers. The system administrator has some control over how printer resources are used, as shown in the Print Spooler Utilities Management menu:

```
PRINT SPOOLER UTILITIES MANAGEMENT

1 paccept        have a line printer accept print jobs
2 lpreject       have a line printer reject print jobs
3 lpremove       remove a line printer from the system
4 lpsetup        add line printer
5 lpstart        start line printer scheduler
6 lpstop         stop line printer scheduler

Enter a number, a name, the initial part of a name, or
? or <number>? for HELP,  ^ to GO BACK,  q to QUIT:
```

VP/ix, the other application shown on the Package Management menu, allows DOS to run as a task under Unix. Through the VP/ix Management menu, the system administrator can control which users will be able to use VP/ix. If your organization maintains both DOS and Unix applications, VP/ix provides a convenient way to operate on both from the same terminal.

The Software Management Menu

The Software Management menu automatically installs or removes applications from a Unix system, if the application was specifically written for automatic installation. The Software Management menu is shown below:

```
SOFTWARE MANAGEMENT

1 installpkg   install new software package onto built-in disk
2 listpkg      list packages already installed
3 removepkg    remove previously installed package from built-in disk
4 runpkg       run software package without installing it

Enter a number, a name, the initial part of a name, or
? or <number>? for HELP,  ^ to GO BACK,  q to QUIT:
```

The System Setup Menu

With the System Setup menu, the system administrator can set system and administrative passwords that protect the system from interference by unauthorized users. In addition, the system node name and the date and time can be set. The node name is important when your system is connected, either directly or through a modem, to other Unix systems. The System Setup menu is shown below:

```
              SYSTEM SETUP

  1 admpasswd  assign or change administrative passwords
  2 datetime   set the date, time, time zone and daylight savings time
  3 nodename   set the node name of this machine
  4 setup      set up your machine the very first time
  5 syspasswd  assign system passwords

Enter a number, a name, the initial part of a name, or
? or <number>? for HELP,  ^ to GO BACK,  q to QUIT:
```

TTY Management Menu

The TTY Management menu allows you to set or change the parameters on your terminals. As your organization changes, the number and characteristics of the terminals you use with your Unix system may need to change as well. The TTY Management menu makes this process relatively straightforward:

```
              TTY MANAGEMENT

  1 lineset    show tty line settings and hunt sequences
  2 mklineset  create new tty line settings and hunt sequences
  3 modtty     show and optionally modify characteristics of tty lines
  4 sunterm    change number of active SunRiver Stations
  5 virtterm   change number of virtual terminals

Enter a number, a name, the initial part of a name, or
? or <number>? for HELP,  ^ to GO BACK,  q to QUIT:
```

User Management Menu

The User Management menu is used by the system administrator to add and delete users and user groups from the system. When you add a new user, you are prompted for the user's name, login ID, group ID, and password. Encourage new users to change their passwords as soon as possible. Once a user login is established, the associated password should be changed from time to time. If an unauthorized user should ever gain access to a valid password, it will work only for a limited time before being changed.

The following display shows the user management functions available:

```
        USER MANAGEMENT

  1 addgroup      add a group to the system
  2 adduser       add a user to the system
  3 delgroup      delete a group from the system
  4 deluser       delete a user from the system
  5 lsgroup       list groups in the system
  6 lsuser        list users in the system
  7 modadduser    modify defaults used by adduser
  8 modgroup      menu of commands to modify group attributes
  9 moduser       menu of commands to modify a user's login

Enter a number, a name, the initial part of a name, or
? or <number>? for HELP,  ^ to GO BACK,  q to QUIT:
```

Setting Up Accounts for Groups and Users

At a small installation with relatively few users, you may not want to go to the trouble of setting up groups of users. On larger systems where the requirements of one user are similar to those of several others, but different from those of everybody else, you may want to create a group for a cluster of people with common needs and interests. For example, several people in the sales department may need access to customer files and sales-transaction files. These sensitive files should not be available to employees from other departments who do not have a legitimate need to know the information. Similarly, employees in the human resources department require access to the company's personnel files, which contain salary information and other confidential material. People in the sales department should not have access to this data. The two groups can be kept separate by creating a group for each, then placing the appropriate users into each group.

To create a group, select **1 addgroup** from the user management menu. A dialogue like the following will ensue:

```
Anytime you want to quit, type "q".
If you are not sure how to answer any prompt, type "?" for help,
or see the Owner/Operator Manual.

If a default appears in the question, press <return> for the default.

Enter group name [?, q]:   sales
Enter group ID number (default 100) [?, q]:

This is the information for the new group:
        Group name:     sales
        group ID        100

Do you want to install, edit, or skip this entry? [i, e, s, q]: i
Group installed.
Do you want to add another group? [y, n, q]
```

After you have added all the groups that you will need initially, add individual users
with **2 adduser** (the second option on the User Management menu). A typical
dialogue might be as follows:

```
Anytime you want to quit, type "q".
If you are not sure how to answer any prompt, type "?" for help,
or see the Owner/Operator Manual.

If a default appears in the question, press <return> for the default.

Enter user's full name [?, q]:  Daryl Alsop
Enter user's login ID [?, q]:    daryl
Enter user ID number (default 102) [?, q]:
Enter group ID number or group name
(default 1) [?, q]:  sales
Enter user's login (home) directory name.
(default '/usr/daryl') [?, q]:

This is the information for the new login:
        User's name:     Daryl Alsop
        login ID:        daryl
        user ID:         102
        group ID:        100     (sales)
        home directory:  /usr/daryl

Do you want to install, edit, or skip this entry [i, e, s, q]? i
Login installed.
Do you want to give the user a password? [y, n] y
New password:
Re-enter new password:
Do you want to add another login? [y, n, q]
```

You can add the rest of the users in the **sales** group, then install the users that belong to the **human** group. Now you can restrict access to customer data to members of the **sales** group, and access to personnel data to members of the **human** group.

Installing New Software

The software-installation facility under the Software Management menu makes the installation of even a large software system a simple task. If the package is delivered on multiple floppy disks, the installation facility prompts you to insert each one into the system floppy drive in turn. The contents of the diskettes are copied onto the system fixed disk, with subdirectories created on the fly, as needed. You do not need to know anything about the application to install it, only how to insert diskettes.

Formatting Floppy Disks

Chapter 4 described how to format a floppy disk using the **format** command. This job can also be performed from the Disk Management menu. The system asks whether you want to verify the format or not, then prompts you for diskette type (1.2-megabyte, 1.44-megabyte, 360-kilobyte, or 720-kilobyte). After you respond, it asks you to insert the diskette and press [Enter]. It then proceeds to format the diskette.

Backing Up

The backup of files contained on the system fixed disk is controlled from the File Management menu. When you select the **backup** option, you are asked which file systems you want to back up and whether you want to do a complete or an incremental backup. (You must have performed at least one complete backup before the system will allow you to do an incremental backup.) After specifying complete or incremental, enter the drive and diskette type you will use. Be sure you have enough formatted diskettes available to contain the entire backup before you start. As each diskette fills up, the system will prompt you to insert another.

A complete backup may take quite a while, so be prepared. Even if your application files do not take up much space, the Unix system itself is large, and will take a long time to copy.

Creating a File System on a Diskette

If a formatted diskette is to be used as a backup medium, it does not require any further preparation. However, if you want to store files on it that are directly accessible to Unix, you must create a file system on the diskette. To do this, choose **5 makefsys** on the Disk Management menu.

First, you must specify the drive and medium size; you are then prompted to insert the appropriate formatted diskette into the designated drive. Next, you are prompted for a label name for the new file system. The label name may be no more than six characters. After specifying the label name, you will be prompted for a file system name and the maximum number of files and directories that the diskette will be called upon to hold. The system will then proceed to build a file system on the diskette. The process takes several minutes. When it is complete, the system will ask you whether you want to leave the system mounted. If you say yes, a message will confirm that the diskette's file system is mounted, and warn you not to remove the diskette without first unmounting the file system on it. The diskette has been mounted as a subdirectory of the **root** directory, with the name that you gave to the file system when you created it.

Mounting and Unmounting a Removable Media File System

Two other options on the Disk Management menu are **7 mountfsys** and **8 umountfsys**, which mount and unmount a diskette file system, respectively. (Of course, diskette-based file systems can also be mounted and unmounted using Unix commands explained in chapter 4.) To mount a floppy-based file system from the Disk Management menu, you must first specify the drive and the capacity of the diskette that you intend to use. You will then be prompted to insert the diskette. The system will read the diskette label and file-system name and ask you to confirm that this is indeed the file system you want to mount. After you confirm, the file system will be mounted, and logically become a part of the file system on your hard disk.

The procedure for unmounting a file system, using **8 umountfsys,** is similar. However, Unix will not unmount a "busy" file system, that is, if any of the files in that system are currently in use or if any user's current directory is contained in that file system. All users must stop using the file system on a diskette before you can unmount it.

Assigning a Node Name to your System

The System Setup submenu of the System Management menu provides an easy way for you to change passwords for system and administrative files, as well as to set the correct date and time. In addition, it allows you to change the node name assigned to your system.

When you first installed your system, it was assigned a default node name. This is not very helpful, because if all systems retained the default node name, any attempt to communicate would cause confusion. If there is any chance that your Unix system will ever communicate with another one, you should change the node name to something unique. Select **3 nodename** from the System Setup submenu. The system will tell you what the current node name is and ask you if you want to change it. Answer yes, enter the new node name, and the change will be made.

SHUTTING THE SYSTEM DOWN

Many system administration tasks do not appear on the system administration menu. One of them is shutting down the system in an orderly manner.

If you were to turn a single-user DOS system's power off when it was waiting at the DOS prompt, no harm would be done. There would be no files open, and no operations would be in progress.

This is not the case with Unix. There are always files open, and operations are always in progress, even if no users are active. A specific shutdown procedure must be followed before a Unix system can safely be powered down. If power to a Unix system is accidentally interrupted, you must go through a file-salvaging procedure before resuming normal operations. For this reason, it is more important to install an uninterruptible power supply (UPS) on a Unix system than it is for a DOS system.

The routine that initiates an orderly shutdown of the system is called **/etc/shutdown.** It can be invoked only by the superuser at the console, and only from the **root** directory. When you issue the **shutdown** command, the system broadcasts a message to all users, warning them of imminent system shutdown. They are instructed to log out immediately to avoid damage to their files. After the broadcast, the system asks the superuser for confirmation of a shutdown, then proceeds with the shutdown.

An important part of the shutdown procedure is the use of the **sync** command to flush all buffers to disk. This assures that disk files are updated. Once the disk has been updated, the system can safely be turned off or rebooted.

SUMMARY

The system administrator bears the ultimate responsibility for the integrity and performance of a Unix system. This responsibility entails the power to take any action necessary to insure that the system operates as it should and that all users receive the service they need.

When the system administrator, or a designated alternate, logs in as **root**, he or she becomes the superuser and assumes broad powers. The superuser may use the system administration shell to perform a number of important system maintenance tasks, or may perform them directly using standard Unix commands. Many of the commands that perform these maintenance functions can be executed only by the superuser.

Chapter 14

Running DOS as a Unix Task

Many Unix users want to continue to operate their existing DOS systems. Even though Unix is substantially more powerful than DOS, it does not make sense to stop using DOS simply because a new Unix system has been acquired. There is a tremendous base of application software available for DOS that dwarfs the number of packages running under Unix. Many of these applications would be difficult or impossible to convert to Unix. As a result, organizations with a large investment in DOS applications naturally want to retain them, even if they develop all their new applications under Unix.

The ideal situation would be to run both DOS and Unix applications on the same computer, sharing files between the two operating systems. This is not possible with native DOS and native Unix, since they have incompatible file structures. However, it can be achieved on Intel 386- and 486-based machines using a DOS emulator called VP/ix.

VP/IX

VP/ix was developed by Phoenix Technologies and is marketed by both The Santa Cruz Operation and Interactive Systems Corporation as an adjunct to their 386-based Unix operating systems. It emulates DOS 3.3 and contains enhancements that facilitate its use within a Unix system.

VP/ix is intended to allow Unix users to run any application that can be run under DOS 3.3. The user can switch seamlessly back and forth between Unix and DOS, and can even issue one operating system's commands while ostensibly functioning in the other operating system's environment.

Although VP/ix is a very accurate emulation of MS-DOS Version 3.3, there are some differences. Like any emulation, VP/ix does not run as fast as native DOS would run on the same machine. For most users, this should not be a problem, as the primary applications will be running under Unix. The main purpose of VP/ix is to allow older applications that were developed under DOS to continue to run. For such applications, performance is less of an issue than is the ability to share information with the new Unix programs.

Installing and Running VP/ix

VP/ix is installed like any commercial application, using the System Administration menu. Any user can switch into DOS emulation mode by entering the **vpix** command. The VP/ix DOS prompt will appear, and you can now run DOS applications without leaving the Unix system.

The Z Drive

VP/ix takes the file system within which it is contained, including unused space, and treats it as a virtual disk drive. This virtual disk drive, called drive Z, is the default drive of the VP/ix environment. VP/ix may have other drives available to it, both hard and flexible, but it can share files with the host Unix system only through drive Z.

The directories and paths on the Z drive are the same as the corresponding directories and paths on the host Unix file system, except for the symbols that separate path elements. Unix uses forward slashes (/) for this purpose, while VP/ix uses backslashes (\). Thus, a user whose home directory under Unix is **/usr/allen** has a corresponding home directory under VP/ix of **Z:\USR\ALLEN**. You can move about among directories on the Z drive exactly as you would on a real drive on a native DOS system.

The VP/ix Interface Menu

You can fully utilize VP/ix by issuing DOS or Unix commands at the DOS prompt. For your convenience, a short menu of commonly needed functions is provided. Depending on the kind of keyboard you have, you can display the menu either by pressing [Alt-SysReq] or [Alt-SysReq-m]. The following menu will appear:

```
(Esc)ape menu
(F)loppy release
(P)rinter flush
(Q)uit VP/ix
(R)eset VP/ix
(S)ound is ON
(C)lose serial
(E)nter shell
```

You may make only one selection from the menu. The menu will disappear, and the function you selected will be carried out.

(Esc)ape menu

This option returns you immediately to the VP/ix DOS prompt.

(F)loppy release

VP/ix is part of a multiuser Unix system on which resources such as floppy-disk drives must be shared. When you first use a floppy drive, VP/ix reserves it for your exclusive use. When finished with the drive, you must release it so that other users may have access to it. As a courtesy to other users, always release floppy drives as soon as you are through with them. When you quit VP/ix, any floppies that you have reserved are automatically released.

(P)rinter flush

When you execute a command under VP/ix that would normally result in printed output, that output is not automatically sent to the print spooler. It is stored in the VP/ix print buffer, which must be *flushed* to the spooler before the print job will be scheduled for printing. The print buffer is automatically flushed when you quit VP/ix.

(Q)uit VP/ix

Selecting this option releases all resources such as floppy drives and serial ports, flushes the print buffer, and returns you to the Unix shell from which you called VP/ix. The screen is restored to what it was when you called VP/ix. Issuing the quit command at the DOS prompt has the same effect.

(R)eset VP/ix

This option reboots VP/ix. It has the same effect as pressing [Ctrl-Alt-Del] on a native DOS system. Only VP/ix is rebooted, not the hardware or the Unix system.

(S)ound is ON/(S)ound is OFF Toggle

You can disable the computer's tone generator by toggling this option to OFF. Restore the sound by toggling it to ON.

(C)lose serial

Once a user accesses a serial port, the system reserves that port for the user's exclusive use. The port can be released either by selecting this option or by quitting the VP/ix environment.

(E)nter shell

This option invokes a new Unix shell and places you into it. Both VP/ix and the Unix shell that called it are suspended, rather than terminated. You can return to VP/ix by exiting the new Unix shell normally. As always, quitting VP/ix will return you to your original Unix shell.

Running a DOS Application

To run a DOS application under VP/ix, you cannot just insert a DOS diskette into a 386 system running Unix, because DOS and Unix file formats are incompatible. The best solution is to send the application's files from a DOS machine to your Unix machine via a serial port.

Once all needed files for a DOS application are resident on your Z drive or on one of the other drives available to you, you can execute the application just as in a native DOS environment. Nearly all DOS applications will run without any problem. A few, generally those such as the Norton Utilities that exercise low-level control over the system hardware, will not run properly under the VP/ix emulation.

Printing

Printing under VP/ix is much like printing under native DOS, with one major exception. Rather than going directly to the printer, output is sent to a buffer in memory. When the buffer is full, its contents are sent on to the print spooler, which prints the output when a printer becomes available. You can force the contents of the buffer to be sent to the spooler either by selecting the (**P**)rinter flush option from the VP/ix Interface menu or by quitting VP/ix. Because output is sent in large chunks to the print spooler, if you flush the buffer too soon after sending output to it, your printed output may be split into several pieces. Avoid flushing the buffer until you are finished outputting text.

Returning to Unix from VP/ix

When you are finished using VP/ix, you can return to your original Unix shell by selecting (**Q**)uit VP/ix from the VP/ix Interface menu. Your screen will be restored to what it was when you invoked VP/ix. A second way to return to your original Unix shell is to enter the **quit** command at the VP/ix DOS prompt. You will be returned to your original shell, but the screen will not be restored to its previous state.

MULTIUSER DOS

Since DOS is a single-user operating system, multiuser operation is not possible on a "stock" DOS system. But since VP/ix runs as a task under multiuser Unix, and since any number of users can simultaneously run a VP/ix task, the equivalent of a multiuser DOS has been created. In this way, VP/ix provides a new dimension to DOS operational capability.

DOS AND UNIX FILE SYSTEM DIFFERENCES

Although there are many similarities between DOS files and Unix files, their differences are enough to make them incompatible. For one thing, DOS allows a file name to be no more than eight characters, with a three-character extension, and does not distinguish between upper- and lowercase characters in file names. Unix allows file names to be more than eight characters, does not use an extension, and does distinguish between upper- and lowercase characters in file names.

Displaying File-Access Permissions

Associated with each Unix file are access permissions that specify who has permission to read, write, and execute the file (see chapter 6 for an explation of file-access permissions). Any multiuser system should have at least this minimal level of security. Single-user DOS has no file-security system whatsoever. This is a serious deficiency, since even a single-user operating system can be accessed by different people at different times.

Although there is no provision on a DOS **dir** display to show access permissions, you can display this information with the VP/ix **xdir** command. This command also shows the full Unix name of files whose names are more than eight characters long or are in some other way illegal under DOS.

Converting Files from One Format to the Other

Because of the differences in file structure, files designed to be run with DOS have to be converted to Unix format before they can be used with VP/ix. VP/ix includes utilities that convert DOS files into Unix format and Unix files into DOS format. Other utilities change DOS path names to the equivalent Unix path names, and vice versa.

ASCII files, also known as text files, are converted with the VP/ix **copy** command. The /**d** option with this command copies a Unix-format file into DOS format, and the /**u** option copies a DOS-format file into Unix format.

The **lef** command changes a file into the other format. Thus, it changes a DOS file into a Unix file, and a Unix file into a DOS file. The **lef** command can be used for both ASCII and non-ASCII files.

DOS AND UNIX TOGETHER

VP/ix is more than just a DOS emulator running as a task under Unix. It is capable of running standard Unix commands as well as DOS commands. Furthermore, you may run DOS programs directly from the Unix prompt. Unix is able to recognize a DOS application and automatically invokes VP/ix before trying to execute it.

Using DOS Commands from the Unix Prompt

You may use DOS commands directly from the Unix prompt. However, since the system must go through an extra level of interpretation, its response time will be slower than if you were issuing Unix commands when in the Unix shell and DOS commands when in VP/ix.

Another thing to watch out for is that some DOS syntax will be misinterpreted by the Unix shell. If your DOS command contains an argument with a wildcard (? or *) or a backslash (\), you must enclose the entire argument in single quotes ('). This will prevent the Unix shell from "seeing" what is in the argument and taking the wrong action.

Running DOS Applications from the Unix Prompt

You can also run entire DOS applications from the Unix prompt. VP/ix will be automatically invoked and the VP/ix Interface menu will be available. The application must be resident on hard disk; DOS applications stored on floppy disk may not be run from the Unix prompt. When you have finished running the DOS application, exit it normally to return to the Unix prompt.

Running a Unix Shell from VP/ix

Just as VP/ix creates a DOS shell that can be invoked from within a Unix shell, it is possible to invoke a new Unix shell from within the VP/ix DOS shell. The VP/ix session is suspended while the new Unix shell is active. When you are finished with the Unix shell and type the **exit** command (or [Ctrl-d]), your VP/ix shell is reactivated. The VP/ix screen that was displayed before you invoked the new Unix shell is restored.

Using Unix Commands from the DOS Prompt

Just as you can issue DOS commands from the Unix prompt, you can issue Unix commands from the DOS prompt. Once again, performance will suffer, since VP/ix has to determine that the commands it receives are Unix commands and then pass the commands on to Unix for execution.

When issuing Unix commands, be sure to use Unix syntax, even if you are in the VP/ix environment. Similarly, DOS commands should use only DOS syntax, even in a Unix shell. Note also that a Unix command executed from within the VP/ix shell can access only files located on the Z drive. The Z drive is the only place where DOS and Unix have access to the same files.

Combining DOS and Unix Commands in a Pipeline

Both DOS and Unix support pipelines, and they use the same symbol to denote a pipe. With VP/ix, you can build a pipeline using commands from both DOS and Unix. For example, the output of a DOS command can be fed into the input of a Unix command, and that output can then be fed back into a DOS command. All the commands will be interpreted properly. This lets you achieve a result using the most convenient commands.

DIFFERENCES BETWEEN VP/IX
DOS AND NATIVE DOS

Because VP/ix is an emulation running on top of a Unix system, there are a few differences between VP/ix DOS and a standard implementation of DOS running in native mode. Unix disk files are different from DOS disk files, so some DOS commands that deal with disks will not work the same as they do in a native DOS system.

The DOS **format** command can be used to format both flexible disks and hard disks; under VP/ix, **format** can be used only with flexible disks. The DOS **chkdsk** command checks the status of the file system on a hard or flexible disk; under VP/ix, **chkdsk** will not work with the Z drive, since the Z drive contains a Unix file system rather than a DOS file system. As noted earlier in this chapter, the VP/ix **copy** command can convert files from DOS to Unix format and from Unix to DOS format, in addition to performing the normal functions of the DOS **copy** command.

SUMMARY

VP/ix, available as an option on several popular 386-based Unix systems, allows users to maintain both DOS and Unix code. Not only can DOS and Unix applications coexist on the same machine, but they may also share files.

VP/ix is an emulation of DOS 3.3 that runs under Unix just like any other application. It reidentifies the current Unix file system as drive Z and can manipulate any files found there.

You can execute both DOS and Unix commands in the VP/ix environment, and the VP/ix Interface menu gives you instant access to several commonly used commands. One of these commands opens up a new Unix shell and suspends the VP/ix shell until your work in the new Unix shell is complete.

The procedure for executing a DOS application under VP/ix is the same as it is under native DOS. Printing is handled differently, however. Print output is buffered in memory before being sent to the printer.

There are some differences between the file structure of DOS and that of Unix; one is that Unix files have file-access permissions for security purposes, while DOS files do not. Conversion utilities are provided with VP/ix.

VP/ix goes beyond mere DOS emulation; it can mix DOS and Unix commands. DOS commands may be issued from the Unix prompt and Unix commands may be issued from the DOS prompt. It is even possible to use a pipeline that mixes DOS and Unix commands on a single command line, which can be very handy for a user conversant with both DOS batch language and the Unix command set.

Chapter 15

Printing

There are important similarities as well as important differences between the way printing is handled under Unix and the way it is handled under DOS. As far as hardware is concerned, the similarities predominate. Printer and interface requirements are identical for the two operating systems. As long as each system has an appropriate device driver, the printers you have set up for one operating system should work equally well with the other.

Some printers are designed to be connected to a parallel interface, and others require a serial interface. The specific device driver attached to the operating system deals with these differences. The operating system kernel, be it DOS or Unix, simply sends a stream of data to the appropriate port.

With respect to print commands, DOS and Unix differ considerably. The DOS **print** command is rudimentary compared to the elaborate system in Unix. One reason is that Unix, being a multiuser operating system, needs a more complex system to handle multiple users sending jobs to the printer at the same time. Another reason is that Unix has always been more oriented toward producing high-quality printed output than has DOS. With its roots in large computers, Unix was heavily used by the publishing industry for years before anyone ever heard of desktop publishing on personal computers. Many sophisticated features developed for publishing and other text-handling applications are built right into the Unix operating system.

THE pr COMMAND

There is no command or combination of commands in DOS that corresponds to the Unix **pr** command. The **pr** command takes a text file as input, formats it, then sends it to standard output. Its many options give you considerable control over the form of the output.

The most frequently used options are those that paginate the text and divide it into multiple columns. One option merges multiple files, like the **cat** command, before sending them to the printer. The merge option is incompatible with the multicolumn option. Other than that, options may be combined in any way desired. Table 15-1 on the next page displays the **pr** command options.

The **pr** command is primarily a document-formatting command. It does not direct output to a printer. Printing is the province of the LP print service.

THE LP PRINT SERVICE

The job of the LP print service is to efficiently schedule print jobs coming in from multiple users and send them to the appropriate printers. The heart of this rather complex system is the *scheduler,* **lpsched**.

The Print Scheduler

The scheduler, also known as the spooler, is a *demon* process. (Demons are processes that run continuously in the background, performing some sort of service for the system.) It is the scheduler's job to see that all print requests are handled as quickly

*Table 15-1 Options available with the **pr** command*

OPTION	FUNCTION
+*page*	Begin printing on page number *page* (default is 1).
−*column*	Print output in *column* columns (default is 1).
-a	Prints multicolumn output across the page in rowwise rather than columnwise fashion.
-m	Merge up to eight files and print them all sequentially. This option is available for single-column output only.
-d	Double-space output.
-e*ck*	Expand input tabs into spaces, with an interval of *k* characters between tabs.
-i*ck*	Replace spaces in output with tabs wherever possible, with an interval of *k* characters between tabs.
-n*ck*	Start each line of output with a sequentially incrementing line number.
-w*width*	Set line width for a multicolumn output.
-o*offset*	Indent output by *offset* character positions.
-l*length*	Set page length to *length* lines.
-h*header*	Print the text string *header* at the top of each page of the printed output.
-p	Pause between pages.
-f	Use form feed to go to next page rather than using a series of line feeds.
-r	Do not print diagnostic reports on files that will not open.
-t	Do not put a header or trailer on a page of output. Cease printing at the end of text, rather than appending line feeds to reach the end of the page.
-s*separator*	Use the single-character *separator,* rather than blank spaces to separate columns in a multi-column document.

and accurately as possible. It arbitrates between print requests that are received at the same time, and assures that each print job is unaffected by other print jobs competing for the system's printers.

The scheduler is automatically activated when the system is booted. However, certain events may turn the scheduler off. When this happens, nothing can be printed. The **lpsched** command will start the scheduler running again. The **lpsched** command is normally located in the **/usr/lib** directory, along with several other LP print-service commands usually used by the superuser. The LP print-service commands available to ordinary users are stored in **/usr/bin**.

The complementary command to **/usr/lib/lpsched** is **/usr/lib/lpshut,** which turns off the scheduler and causes all currently active print jobs to stop printing. Ordinary users usually have permission to issue both the **lpsched** and the **lpshut** commands, as well as the other printer-related commands in the **/usr/lib** directory. However, since most users do not have that directory included in their search path, they must specify the full path and file name when invoking the **lpsched** and **lpshut** commands.

The **lpmove** command, related to **lpsched** and **lpshut**, moves print requests from one printer to another. If jobs are stacking up in one printer queue, you may use **lpmove** to move some of them to another printer on the system. Once the queued-up jobs have been completed, you can shut down the LP print-service system, if desired, without causing major disruption.

The lp Command

Although the LP print service includes a number of commands (most beginning with the letters *lp*), only the **lp** command actually causes something to be printed. Its many options let you customize your printout in a variety of ways.

If you specify only the name of the file to be printed, with no options, **lp** will queue the file to the first available printer. With options, you can specify which printer will perform the job, how many copies it will print, and a number of other things. Table 15-2 summarizes the options available.

You can use the **cancel** command to abort a print request that has not yet been completed. Specifying either the job's request ID or the printer on which it is being printed.

*Table 15-2 Options for the **lp** command*

OPTION	DESCRIPTION
-c	Makes copies of document files as soon as the print request is made. These copies are used to make the printout. Any changes made to the original files after the print request will not be reflected in the printout.
-d *dest*	Specifies a particular printer or class of printers as the destination of this print request.
-f *formname*	Prompts the operator to mount the specified form in the destination printer.
-H *spclhndlng*	Requests special handling of this print request. Possible arguments are **hold**, **resume**, and **immediate**. **hold** suspends the printout. **resume** reinserts a suspended job into the queue. **immediate** causes this job to be printed next.
-m	Sends mail to the user upon completion of the print job.
-n *number*	Directs the system to print the specified number copies of the job.
-o *option*	Specifies printer-dependent options, such as page length, page width, lines per inch, and characters per inch, as well as the removal of normal banner pages and form feeds between files.
-P *page-list*	Directs the system to print only the specified pages.
-q *priority*	Assigns the specified priority (between 0 and 39) to this job. 0 is the highest; 20 is the default.
-s	Suppresses messages normally returned from **lp** to standard output.
-S *char set*	Requests that the printout be made with the specified character set.
-t *title*	Causes the specified title to be printed on the banner page at the top of the print job.
-T *contenttype*	Restricts printout to printers that support the specified content type.
-w	Informs the user of the completion of printing with a message on the user's terminal. If the user is not logged in, mail is sent instead.
-y *modelist*	Causes printout to be made according to the specified print modes.

The lpstat Command

You can learn the status of the print system, and of any jobs that are in the queue or currently being printed, by using the **lpstat** command and its options. For example, you may use **lpstat** to see what printers are available for use and where your own job stands in the queue. If a job you submitted no longer shows up in the **lpstat** display, then it must have finished printing.

When issued without arguments, **lpstat** gives you information about only your own jobs. For example, if you enter a print request, then ask for status before it starts printing, a dialogue like the following would take place:

```
$ lp /etc/profile
request id is okidata-13 (1 file)
$lpstat
okidata-13              root              783    Sep  6 18:39
$
```

After printing commences, another invocation of **lpstat** yields a slightly different display, as shown in the following:

```
$lpstat
okidata-13              root         783    Sep  6 18:39 on okidata
```

On the right, the display shows the name of the printer that is currently printing the job. After printing is complete, another invocation of **lpstat** produces no output. This shows that you currently have no active print jobs.

If you want complete information about the status of the print system, use the **-t** option, as shown in the following:

```
$ lpstat -t
scheduler is running
system default destination: okidata
device for okidata: /dev/lp1
okidata accepting requests since Thu Jul 20 21:43:57 1989
printer okidata is idle. enabled since Thu Jul 20 21:43:58 1989. avail.
$
```

Other options provide information about character sets, print wheels, and the availability of specified forms on a printer, as well as full descriptions of printer configurations.

The enable and disable Commands

You can use **enable** and its opposite, **disable**, to control whether specified printers will accept jobs. A typical usage would be to disable a printer that needs a new ribbon, then enable it when the replacement has been made. If a printer is disabled in the middle of a task, the entire job will be printed when the printer is enabled.

The lpadmin Command

The **lpadmin** command is used to add printers to, or remove them from, the system. Generally, only the system administrator will use it. It is also used to specify the system's default printer. A print job without a specified destination will be printed on the default printer, if it is available.

The **lpadmin** command tells the system all it needs to know about a new printer. It also specifies the form of the printed output, including page length, page width, characters per inch, and lines per inch. Many system administrators will not need to learn the intricacies of the **lpadmin** command, since the addition and removal of printers is one of the jobs handled by the system administrator's shell on most systems. The menu-driven shell calls upon the **lpadmin** command, but spares the user from the syntactical details.

The accept and reject Commands

There is one more layer of control over printer operation. Even when a printer is enabled and the scheduler is running, it still may not be able to print anything. If the **reject** command has been issued for a specified printer, it will reject all print requests until the **accept** command it executed for it.

SUMMARY

The operating system is much more involved in the production of printed output under Unix than it is under DOS. The Unix **pr** command provides formatting for a document file, which is lacking in DOS. To achieve similar formatting in a DOS environment, you would need to use a text processing application program.

Since Unix is a multiuser system, there must be a mechanism for determining who gets the printers and when. The printed output generated for each user must not be affected by other print jobs. This responsibility is assumed by the scheduler, also known as either the spooler or the print demon. Once started, the scheduler runs continuously in the background, handling print requests as they occur.

The **lp** command is the only LP print-service command that actually causes the contents of a text file to be printed on paper. The large number of options available with **lp** gives a user considerable control over the exact form of the printout.

Other commands that make up the LP print-service system perform additional functions. The **lpstat** command, for example, keeps you apprised of the status of jobs waiting to be printed or currently being printed. The **enable, disable, accept,** and **reject** commands help control the availability of system printers. On a more fundamental level, the **lpadmin** command installs and configures new printers and removes printers that are no longer needed.

The LP print service provides Unix users with a flexible and reliable method of obtaining hard copy, even in large installations with many users.

## Chapter 16

Text Formatting

U sers coming to Unix from the DOS world are familiar with desktop publishing using applications such as Ventura Publisher and Aldus PageMaker. With these applications, a user of moderate skill can produce camera-ready output that may be sent directly to a typesetting machine.

One of the reasons users who are not professional typesetters can achieve very good results is that these packages feature a WYSIWYG interface. WYSIWYG (pronounced wiz-ee-wig) stands for "What You See Is What You Get." In a WYSIWYG system, the document shown on the screen during the formatting operation is a very close approximation of what the finished output will look like on paper. Different fonts and type sizes, mathematical symbols, and even illustrations are all shown as they will appear in the final document. This allows the user to refine a document until it looks just right before committing it to paper.

Unix was widely used for text formatting long before the WYSIWYG interface was invented. In Unix's early days, high-resolution graphics terminals were rare and expensive. Text formatting was done on standard character-based terminals. Unix borrowed the system, then in widespread use in the publishing industry, of interspersing formatting commands throughout the body of a document. When the file was sent to a printer or typesetter, the formatting commands were recognized as such and executed, rather than printed as text.

Users with a background in publishing find this method very natural and are able to produce quite complex documents with it. For PageMaker experts, however, such a command-driven interface may seem to be a step backward.

TEXT FORMATTING: AN EXTRA-COST OPTION

The basic Unix system sold today generally does not include text-formatting software. The traditional Unix text-processing system, with its command-driven interface consists of a collection of programs that can be purchased separately from the operating system. Those who do not need it are not burdened with the extra cost and with the disk space that it takes up.

In the past, if you wanted formatted output, you had no choice but to learn and use the utilities in the text-processing system. They are very powerful, but also quite hard to learn. Because of their complexity, you must use them frequently to maintain your proficiency. If you would like document formatting to be a major part of your job description, it may pay you to become an expert on the Unix text-processing system; if not, you may be better served by one of the WYSIWYG publishing packages that are now available.

THE UNIX TEXT-PROCESSING SYSTEM

The text-processing system includes macros, formatters, and preprocessors. Macros are text-formatting commands that are grouped into *libraries* intended for different types of documents. For example, the **mm** macro system is designed for use with memorandums and letters. The **mv** macro system was especially created for the production of viewgraphs.

The macros supplement the capabilities of the formatters **nroff** and **troff**. The use of the two formatters is very similar. The difference is that the output of **nroff** is designed to be printed on line printers, while **troff** output is intended for typesetting machines or laser printers.

Preprocessors put text into special formats before feeding it to **nroff** or **troff**. For example, one preprocessor puts mathematical expressions into standard mathematical notation. Another preprocessor puts data into a table and draws appropriate boxes around it.

Macros

Macros are commands that perform specialized manipulations on a document in conjunction with one of the formatters. They are grouped into libraries of related functions.

One of the most commonly used collections is **mm**, which is specifically aimed at the production of letters, reports, memorandums, papers, manuals, and books. Table 16-1 lists some of the macros in the **mm** library.

*Table 16-1. Some of the macros in the **mm** library*

FUNCTION	COMMAND
Body of a document	
Set justification	.SA
Start a new paragraph	.P
Create a numbered heading	.H
Create an unnumbered heading	.HU
Label a table	.TB
Start a table	.TS
Start a display	.DS
Label an equation	.EC
Label an exhibit	.EX
Label a figure	.FG
End a display	.DE
Create a floating display	.DF
Format a bulleted list	.BL
Format a dash list	.DL
Format an automatically incremented list	.AL

Table 16-1 (continued)

Specify a list item	.LI
End a list	.LE
Force a page break	.SK
Start formatting a footnote	.FS
End formatting a footnote	.FE
Create a page header	.PH
Create an even-page header	.EH
Create an odd-page header	.OH
Create a page footer	.PF
Create an even-page footer	.EF
Create an odd-page footer	.OF
Use the bold font	.B
Use the italic font	.I
Use the roman font	.R
Change the point size and vertical spacing	.S

Beginning of a formal memorandum

Title	.TL
Author	.AU
Author's title	.AT
Author's firm	.AF
Memorandum type	.MT

Business Letter

Start writer's address	.WA
End writer's address	.WE
Start recipient's address	.IA
End recipient's address	.IE
Letter type	.LT
Letter options	.LO

End of a document

Formal closing	.FC
Signature block	.SG
Approval line	.AV

When you combine the macros in the **mm** library with either **nroff** or **troff**, you will be able to perform professional-quality formatting for most types of documents.

Formatters

The text formatters provide the basic tools for formatting raw text. The **nroff** formatter is specifically aimed at formatting text for standard character printers. The **troff** formatter is designed to format text for typesetters and laser printers or other high-quality graphics printers.

In principle, you could format documents using only a formatter. However, formatter commands operate at a low level, making them somewhat difficult to use. Macros and preprocessors are generally used in conjunction with a formatter to arrive at the same result, with a lot less work. The macros and preprocessors automate functions that you would have to do manually if you had only a formatter.

nroff

Everyone wants to produce documents that are well proportioned, balanced, and easy to comprehend. However, typeset quality is not always required; for most jobs, the output of a letter-quality character printer is quite sufficient. The **nroff** formatter combined with the **mm** macro package can give very satisfactory results. For such documents as memorandums, letters, outlines, and reports, these two tools may be all you need. Table 16-2 lists some of the most commonly used commands included in **nroff**.

The fonts available to the **ft** command under **nroff** are generally called *roman, italic,* and *bold*. Roman is the printer's normal font; italic is the printer's normal font underlined; and bold is the printer's normal font double struck.

Embed **nroff** commands in your text file. The dot in the first character position alerts the formatter that this line contains a command to be executed, rather than a line of text to be formatted. Once your text file contains the appropriate formatter commands, perform the formatting function by invoking the **nroff** command as illustrated by the following examples:

```
$ nroff infile.txt  outfile.txt
```

or

```
$ nroff infile.txt | lp
```

*Table 16-2. Some important **nroff** formatting commands*

FUNCTION	COMMAND
Output a blank line	.sp
Indent the next line	.ti
Indent all following lines	.in
Fill the following lines with text	.fi
Do not fill the following lines with text	.nf
Insert a line break rather than filling out a line	.br
Turn hyphenation on	.hy
Specify a character to indicate acceptable hyphenation	.hc
Specify how to hyphenate a word	.hw
Turn hyphenation off	.nh
Center the following text	.ce
Justify margin	.ad
Turn off right justification	.na
Translate one character into another	.tr
Set tabs	.ta
Select a font	.ft
Underline the next line	.ul
Add an offset to the default left margin	.po
Change the length of the following lines	.ll
Change the page length	.pl
Begin a new page	.bp
Specify a page number for the following page	.pn
Keep the following lines together on one page	.ne
Define a string	.ds
Set one of the predefined number registers	.nr
Define a macro	.de

In the first case, the unformatted **infile.txt** is formatted by **nroff** and sent to the new file named **outfile.txt.** In the second case, the unformatted **infile.txt** is formatted by **nroff** and sent directly to the LP print service to be printed on the system's line printer.

The commands included in **nroff** allow fine-tuning of formatting. Each command performs a very simple operation. It may take several such commands to accomplish a job that will be needed repeatedly. For example, you may want to set off a section heading by skipping a line, changing the font for the heading to bold, skipping another line, then changing the font back to normal roman. You can define a macro of your own to perform all of these actions with a single command.

troff

The **troff** formatter offers nearly all of the commands provided by **nroff**, plus others that let you go far beyond anything that **nroff** can do. **nroff** is meant to be used with printers that emulate the output of a typewriter. It therefore has a number of limitations, such as a fixed character set, only one font, fixed character size, and fixed vertical spacing.

troff formats text for typesetting machines, laser printers, and other high-quality graphics devices. With these devices, you can place any character of any size anywhere on the page. You can even create new characters and mix them with the characters from any of the many standard fonts available. The number of fonts you may use depends on your hardware and device drivers rather than on **troff**. The output of the **troff** formatter is acceptable for books and other high quality-publishing tasks. Table 16-3 lists some important **troff** commands.

Table 16-3. Commonly used **troff** *commands*

FUNCTION	COMMAND
Request a font	.ft or \f
Mount a font	.fp
Request a point size	.ps or \s
Request vertical spacing	.vs
Set line spacing	.ls
Specify vertical motion	\v
Specify horizontal motion	\h

Preprocessors

Many types of publishing require you to integrate various elements—besides ordinary text—into a document. These may include such items as tables, mathematical equations, illustrations and graphs. To handle these elements, preprocessors prepare the input data before it is sent to the formatter. Commands are embedded in the text file. The preprocessor recognizes and executes those commands, creating structures that the formatter alone cannot generate. The file is then passed to the formatter, which processes the rest of the document.

Tables may be formatted with both **nroff** and **troff**. Equations, illustrations, and graphs are formatted only with **troff**.

tbl

The **tbl** preprocessor is one of the most commonly used. With it, you can create tables that range from very simple to very complex. When used with **troff**, **tbl** produces typeset-quality tables. You can draw boxes around the data, as well as place horizontal and vertical lines wherever you want them. With **nroff**, you can still draw boxes and lines, but they will be built up out of characters in the standard ASCII set. Lines will be represented by a series of dashes, rather than an unbroken line.

To illustrate the use of the **tbl** preprocessor, create a table showing the average temperature and precipitation during January of a group of small towns around the United States. With your editor, create the following text file:

```
.TS
box;
c c c.
City<Tab>Average<Tab>Average
<Tab>January<Tab>January
<Tab>Temperature<Tab>Precipitation
<Tab>F<Tab>in inches

_

Holly Hill, FL<Tab>61<Tab>2.5 rain
North Granby, CT<Tab>24<Tab>13 snow
Allentown, PA<Tab>32<Tab>6 snow
Hudson, NH<Tab>21<Tab>18 snow
Westminster, CA<Tab>57<Tab>3 rain
.TE
```

<Tab> means "press the [Tab] key." The **.TS** command starts the table, and **.TE** ends it. The **box** instruction draws a box, while the **c c c** command indicates that there are three columns and they are all to be centered. The underscore (_) calls for a horizontal line below the headings.

The following command will turn this information into a table and store it in a file:

```
tbl -TX avetemp|nroff -mm -Tlp|col  avetemp.tbl
```

In this case you are using **nroff** to do the formatting for a line printer. The resulting table will look like the following:

City	Average January Temperature F	Average January Precipitation in inches
Holly Hill, FL	61	2.5 rain
North Granby,CT	24	13 snow
Allentown, PA	32	6 snow
Hudson, NH	21	18 snow
Westminster, CA	57	3 rain

You have quite a bit of control over the appearance of the table. For instance, you could have left-justified the **City** column by replacing the **c c c.** command with an **l c c.** command. You can even alter the justification from one line to the next, or specify different fonts for different columns.

By providing an easy way to add good-looking tables to a document, the **tbl** preprocessor is a valuable adjunct to both **nroff** and **troff**.

eqn

The **eqn** preprocessor, designed to be used with **troff**, converts mathematical expressions into standard mathematical notation. It supports all the commonly used mathematical symbols, such as the integral sign and the summation sign, as well as all the letters of the ancient Greek alphabet, subscripts, and superscripts.

An analogous preprocessor named **neqn** performs the same function for **nroff**, but it provides only a draft-quality image of the output of **eqn**. Some line printers that might be used with **neqn** do not even have subscript and superscript capability, and **nroff** can generate only Greek letters and mathematical symbols that are part of the ASCII set. As a result, **neqn** is of limited value. You would probably never want to include its output in a finished document.

An equation may be either embedded in a line of text or set off on a line by itself. The macro pair **.EQ** and **.EN** indicates set-off equations, as illustrated in the following example:

```
.EQ
a = b + 3
.EN
```

The **.EQ** macro marks the beginning of an equation. Everything following is considered a part of the equation, up until **.EN**.

pic

The **pic** preprocessor lets you draw pictures using a library of primitive shapes, such as lines, arrows, circles, ellipses, and boxes. **pic** is useful for drawing such things as block diagrams and flow charts.

Pictures are set off in document files by the macro pair **.PS** and **.PE**, which stand for "picture start" and "picture end." The **pic** processor has its own command language for specifying the elements to be included in a drawing. It works only with **troff**, as **nroff** is not capable of dealing with graphical constructs.

grap

The **grap** preprocessor creates a graph from a set of data points or geometrical figures. You can specify the gradations on the x and the y axes, or **grap** will do it for you automatically. In normal use, the output of **grap** is directed to **pic**, which in turn sends it to **troff**.

The **grap** processor has its own language, used between the **.G1** and **.G2** delimiters. This programming language is rich enough to create all the popular types of graphs. Line graphs, scatter graphs, and bar graphs may be produced, as well as graphs with log-log and semi-log axes. When such graphs are rendered by **troff**, their quality is good enough to appear in published books.

SUMMARY

In the early days of Unix, high-quality text formatting was one of its major applications. Today, there are attractive alternatives to the Unix text-processing system. These newer systems, which feature WYSIWYG interfaces, are capable of producing output equal to that of the Unix text-processing system. They are also much easier for nonprogrammers to learn and use. As a result, the text-processing system is generally not included today in basic Unix systems designed to run on personal computers. Instead, it is available as an extra-cost option.

The principal elements of the Unix text-processing system are the formatters, the macros, and the preprocessors. The formatters **nroff** and **troff** are the workhorses that transfer unformatted text into a document suitable for printing. Macros are gathered together into libraries, such as **mm**. They allow the user to communicate with the formatters at a higher level, making document formatting quicker and easier. Preprocessors insert special constructs, such as tables, equations, pictures, and graphs into the text of a document. The most commonly used preprocessors are **tbl**, **eqn**, **pic**, and **grap**.

With these tools, you should be able to satisfactorily perform any text-processing task, including the production of professional-quality books.

Chapter 17

Software Development

Although Unix is a general-purpose operating system in every sense, and can be used to perform almost any conceivable computing task, it is primarily used as a software-development environment. This is partially due to its origin at AT&T, where it was developed and used almost exclusively for software development. It is also due to Unix's close association with the C language, which is available on virtually every kind of computer.

Applications developed in C under Unix can be easily ported to a wide variety of operating platforms. As a result, most major software companies do all of their development in C, running on a Unix system. The resulting software is then transferred to the target machine, where it is compiled and run. The operating system on the target machine, which may be anything from a microcomputer to a supercomputer, need not be Unix.

THE C STANDARD SUBROUTINE LIBRARY

The modular design of the C language is responsible for much of its flexibility and efficiency. On the other hand, the resulting compartmentalization makes C somewhat more difficult to learn and use than other high-level languages.

Many functions performed directly by other high-level languages are lacking in C. You must invoke subroutines residing in the standard subroutine library in order to perform such functions as string manipulation, arithmetic calculations, and conversions of the representation of numbers. These subroutines are linked into your application at compile time, in effect becoming a part of your application program.

SYSTEM CALLS

System calls are requests that an application makes to the Unix kernel for services that only the operating system can perform. System calls are similar to subroutines in the sense that the application is calling upon an external resource. Unlike subroutines, however, they are not linked into the application. When a system call is made, execution of the application is interrupted and control is transferred to the operating system until the requested operation is completed. Control is then returned to the application, which resumes where it left off.

There are three main types of system calls. One type involves input from, and output to, the "outside world." The outside world may be an I/O device, a pipe, or a file. Typical functions are reading data from a file, writing data to a file, and adding a process to a pipeline. These system calls perform functions that in most cases can be performed adequately by the standard I/O package. Use standard I/O if you can, instead of system calls. System calls tend to be more hardware dependent than is standard I/O; as a result, applications that include such system calls are less portable than those that do not.

The second type of system call retrieves status information about the system or makes a change to the system. Examples are reading the date, getting a user ID, changing the ownership of a file, mounting or unmounting a file system, and changing the current working directory.

Process-control system calls constitute the third category. This important group includes creating a new process, changing the identity of a process, and terminating a process.

Remember that system calls tend to slow down execution. Since the application must be suspended and control transferred to the kernel with every system call, the overhead associated with this transfer is added to the time taken by the execution of the system call itself. If a program makes a great many system calls, they may adversely affect overall performance.

HEADER FILES AND LIBRARIES

Many of the elements an application needs to function properly are not included in the program itself. They are stored somewhere else and referenced in the program.

Definitions and declarations that can apply to multiple program modules are kept in *header files*. These header files are then referenced near the top of a C program module with an **include** directive. The include directive tells the compiler to include the statements in the header file as if they were a part of the application.

A number of header files of general applicability, are included with the Unix software-development system. You can also create your own header files using a text editor. By convention, header file names are given an extension of **.h** and are stored in the **/usr/include** directory. You can store your personal header files in one of your own directories, as long as you include the relative path in the **include** directive you use to invoke it.

Libraries, also called archives, contain modules that are available for inclusion in application programs. These modules are already compiled and stored as object files. The system calls described in the previous section are stored in one such library, called **libc.a** and located in the **/lib** directory.

Libraries are usually given an extension of **.a** (for archive). If you develop libraries of your own, you should store them in the **/usr/lib** directory. The link editor will automatically look there for library routines during compilation of an application.

ERROR HANDLING

When an error occurs during the execution of a C program, the operating system indicates the cause of the error. It returns a value to the program that alerts it to the error, and also places an integer value into the externally declared variable **errno**.

This integer is a code that indicates which operation caused the failure. Your application can read the value of **errno** and decide what action to take. Some errors can be corrected without operator intervention; otherwise, the program writes a message to the console asking the operator to take appropriate action.

THE make COMPILATION CONTROL TOOL

Since C is designed to allow applications to be built up from many program modules that are linked at compile time, there is a potential problem in version control. If you make a change to one module, other modules may be affected. All modules that call the changed module must be recompiled so the change is propagated to all the necessary places. For large applications with highly interdependent modules, this can be very difficult.

A development tool named **make** guarantees the recompilation of all modules affected by a change without recompiling unaffected modules. A description file, usually named **makefile**, informs the **make** utility of the dependencies among modules. **makefile** also contains the commands that actually perform the compilation operation, as well as any associated macro definitions. A file with a modification date earlier than that of a file it depends upon will be recompiled.

THE SOURCE CODE CONTROL SYSTEM (SCCS)

SCCS is a formal and elaborate system for insuring that text files are updated in an orderly manner. Its primary job is to maintain the integrity of program source files over long periods of time, as changes are made by multiple programmers. SCCS enforces several disciplines to keep control of source files.

First, it allows only one copy of the source file to exist. This single master file is encoded in a special SCCS format. It cannot be modified without passing through the controls put in place by SCCS. Since only one master file exists, there is no chance that a programmer could accidentally update an obsolete version, thereby reintroducing program bugs that had already been found and removed.

212

Second, SCCS maintains an "audit trail" of all changes made to the source file since it was placed under the control of SCCS. You can recover any previous version of the file, modify it, and thus create a new variant of the program. This new variant will be controlled as tightly as the original. The two programs are distinguished by being on different branches of the version-number tree. For example, version 1.4 and version 1.3.1 are both descendants of version 1.3. They may both be considered "current" versions, since they terminate different branches of the version number tree.

A third discipline imposed by SCCS has to do with accessibility. The person who first puts a file under the control of SCCS can specify which users may modify it. The danger of file corruption can be greatly reduced by restricting the number of people who can write to it.

The **admin** command is used to create an SCCS master file. The **get** command retrieves a copy of the encoded master file and converts it to standard ASCII form. You may then alter the ASCII file with your text editor.

When you have finished making changes, update the master file with the **delta** command. In spite of its name, **delta** does not actually change the master file. It simply appends the changes (or deltas) to the file. In this way, the original file, or any subsequent version, can be retrieved by a **get** command whose arguments include the desired version number. The necessary deltas will be applied to the original file to produce the requested version.

When **delta** updates an SCCS master file, the ASCII version of the file is automatically deleted. This prevents anyone from making uncontrolled modifications to the program source. You will want to compile the program before you issue the **delta** command. Otherwise, the compiler will not find the file it needs and will issue an error message.

You should not apply the SCCS to a program until it has achieved a relatively stable form. If you put a program under the control of SCCS too soon, you will have to go through a cycle of **get** and **delta** every time you make a minor change. This could considerably slow the debugging process. Furthermore, the SCCS encoded file will grow quite large as it preserves all the changes that have been made throughout its history. Once the file has reached the stage where it is changed only rarely, placing it under SCCS is appropriate.

SUMMARY

One of the primary uses of the Unix operating system has historically been as a development environment for application programs. In many ways, the modular architecture of Unix is optimized for software development, particularly in the C language; this language tends to impose modularity upon programs written with it. By requiring the programmer to go outside the program to subroutines, libraries, and system calls to perform basic functions, the core application remains smaller and more comprehensible. An additional advantage is the fact that commonly used functions need be created only once. Stored in libraries, these functions may be easily included in an application as many times as needed. They also become available to any subsequent applications that may need them.

The C language incorporates a useful error-handling facility. Since error numbers are accessible to the executing application, including appropriate error-recovery code in your application, may allow execution to proceed without operator intervention. If not, the error code will give you a good indication of the cause of the error.

Tools provided with the C software-development system help make the task of software development easier and more consistent. The **make** utility controls the compilation of multimodule software systems when some of the modules have been modified, automatically recompiling only modules affected by the change. The source code control system (SCCS) controls the versions of an application as it undergoes modification over a period of time, preventing updates from being mistakenly made to obsolete versions of a file. It allows, however, a completely new variant of a file to be based on an older version. Not only is the current version of a file maintained by SCCS, but so are all previous versions, each uniquely identified by its SCCS ID number.

Chapter 18

X Windows

In a multiuser, multitasking operating system like Unix, several unrelated activities can be going on at once. It is difficult to keep track of the status of these activities and to interact with them if all you can see on your screen is the current command line and the 23 lines that precede it. The normal character-based display gives you little or no information about the current status of tasks running in the background.

The advent of high-resolution graphics on computers has enabled the development of much more helpful and informative displays. One of the most powerful ideas in the display of computer information is that of *windows*. Windows offer an easy way of viewing data in different formats and of simultaneously viewing several pieces of seemingly unrelated data.

To understand the concept of windows, imagine that all information of possible interest is available within the display terminal. To see any piece of it, you need only open a window that is looking directly at the desired information. You may open as many windows as you wish to keep track of multiple programs. You have the capability of moving the windows around on the screen and resizing them to optimize the overall presentation of information.

A windowing system gives you the ability to rapidly switch your attention from one task to another. This fast *context switching* can markedly improve your productivity when you are interacting with several concurrently executing tasks.

Because of their capabilities and congenial user interface, windowing systems are popular with users. Unfortunately, such systems are resource-intensive, requiring a high-resolution graphics display and a large chunk of system memory. A windowing system also requires more disk space and more CPU cycles than a character-based system. Therefore, a windowing system should be run only on a fairly powerful machine well endowed with main memory and disk storage. A computer that can satisfactorily run a character-based Unix system may be incapable of supporting a windowing environment on top of it.

WHAT IS THE X WINDOW SYSTEM?

The X Window system is a network-based graphics windowing system that was developed at MIT in 1984. The current version is X Version 11, often referred to as X11 or simply X. X has been endorsed by many of the most influential computer manufacturers, including DEC, Hewlett-Packard, Sun, IBM, and AT&T. Implementations of X run on computers manufactured by all these companies.

One of the big advantages of X is that it produces a consistent interface to application developers. Developers who create applications consistent with the X standard do not have to be concerned with the hardware. They can develop an X application on one platform, knowing that it will run on all other machines that support X with little or no modification.

THE X SERVER/CLIENT MODEL

The X Window system is functionally divided into two parts: the *server* and the *clients*. The server is the hardware-specific part of the system; it knows the characteristics of your display, mouse, and keyboard. Clients are the applications; they interface only with the server, so they are not in direct contact with the hardware. Since X is a network-based system, clients need not be running on the same computer as the server. They may be running on completely different types of computers; they have only to conform to the X server/client interface. The server makes all differences in hardware transparent to the client.

THE X DISPLAY

The appearance of an X display will vary from one implementation to another, but some common elements are found in all X systems. The "look and feel" of an X implementation is governed by one of the client processes called the *window manager*. The window manager, like other clients, may or may not be running on the same computer as the server. It allows the user to move windows around on the screen and to resize them.

Figure 18-1 shows a typical X display screen, as implemented by the Motif window manager.

As the example in figure 18-1 shows, windows may overlap. You can bring any one of them to the fore by clicking on any portion of it with the left mouse button. The window border will change color to indicate that it is now the active window.

CHOOSING AND CONFIGURING
AN X DISPLAY SERVER

The server's job is to take input from the keyboard and the mouse, as well as from any clients that are running, and update the screen with new information.

The procedure for choosing and configuring a server will vary somewhat from one implementation of Unix to another. In general, you must tell the system what kind of display, mouse, and keyboard you have. The installation program will display a list of choices and prompt you to select those that correspond to your hardware.

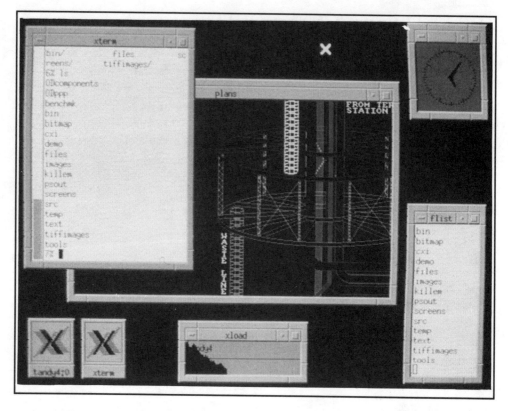

Figure 18-1. X display screen, showing an xterm window, the xclock client, the x load client, two other client windows, and icons representing two more clients

If your mouse, for example, is not listed during the installation procedure, that means that your version of X does not have a driver to support your mouse. You must either add the missing driver to your kernel file system, or switch to a mouse that is supported.

CLIENTS

Any program that runs under the direction of the display server is a client. Several standard clients will be delivered with your X system. You can write additional client programs yourself. If you wish, you can write it so that it takes advantage of all the graphical elements supported by X, and will run in a window as smoothly and seamlessly as do the standard clients. The following sections briefly describe some of the most commonly available standard clients.

The Window Manager

The window manager is your primary tool for manipulating the windows on your screen. With it, you can move windows around on the screen, change their sizes, overlap them, and shuffle overlapping ones so that the desired window is displayed on top. A number of window managers are available that differ in the appearance of the windows and their borders, the form and content of the menus for performing various functions, and the location and appearance of the *widgets* used to perform manipulations. Despite these differences in appearance, however, all window managers perform the same functions. Once you learn how one window manager works, you can learn the details of another in a few minutes.

The examples in this chapter will use the Motif window manager (**mwm**). The Motif interface has been accepted as a standard by the Open Software Foundation (OSF).

The xterm Terminal Emulator

Although the X Window system gives you an attractive high-resolution graphical interface, you may sometimes want to run software that expects to be run from a dumb ASCII terminal. You can emulate such a terminal with **xterm**. Most X implementations provide an **xterm** client that is capable of emulating the DEC VT102 terminal and the Tektronix 4014 terminal; choose whichever is most appropriate for your application. The default emulation is usually VT102. You can run several **xterm** windows at once; some can be VT102 and some Tek 4014.

The xclock Client

The **xclock** client displays the current system time on the screen in either analog or digital format. You can resize its window to make the clock face as large or as small as you like.

The xload Client

The **xload** client gives you a continuously updated graphical display of how heavily the system is loaded. As the processing load increases, the histogram in the **xload** window goes up. As processes complete and resources are idled, the histogram goes down. By looking at **xload** while a specific application is running, you can get a good idea of how resource-intensive it is.

The xcalc Client

The **xcalc** client emulates a handheld scientific calculator. Most implementations of **xcalc** give you a choice of emulations. You can choose one that uses standard algebraic notation like Texas Instrument calculators, reverse notation like Hewlett-Packard calculators, or even one that emulates an analog sliderule. If you are working on a mathematical problem in one of your windows, it is easy to move your mouse over to an **xcalc** window to perform a quick computation. You can then return to your original window, plug in the answer, and proceed with your work.

The xbiff Client —mail box.

The **xbiff** client displays a picture of a rural mailbox. If you have mail waiting in your electronic mailbox, the flag on the box will be up.

The bitmap Client

The **bitmap** client is a graphics editor that allows you to create graphical images by turning bits on and off in a rectangular array. The image you create is transformed into a code fragment that can be included in an application program and used to draw the image on the screen.

STARTING X

There is a command script (its name varies from one implementation of X to another) that starts the X display server, starts the window manager, and opens an **xterm** window. After setting up the paths needed for all X files to be accessible, the script issues an **xinit** command to start the display server and the first client program. Next, it issues an **mwm** or similar command to start the window manager. (You could perform these steps manually, but it is much easier to use a script.) Once the system has been started and the first **xterm** client window is displayed, you can adjust the display to your taste. —display

x init —
mwm
x term —

MANIPULATING WINDOWS WITH WIDGETS

The visual display of a client running in a window, as well as some forms of interaction between the user and a window, are controlled by widgets. Widgets are predefined components, normally found in the X Toolkit, that a programmer uses when building a windowing application to make its interface consistent with all other applications built with the X Toolkit. The specific form of widgets may differ from one implementation of Unix to another, although their respective functions are similar.

Figure 18-2 shows an X display with one **xterm** window open in the SCO Xsight implementation of the Motif window manager.

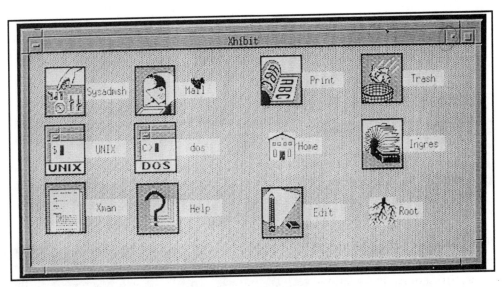

Figure 18-2. X display showing widgets around a window border

The window border is made up of widgets that can move the window or change its size. The title bar at the top of the window is also a widget. By placing the cursor within the title bar and depressing the leftmost mouse button, you can drag the entire window to anywhere on the screen.

The horizontal bar above the title bar is another widget. By placing the cursor within it and depressing the leftmost mouse button, you can move the top edge of the window up or down to make the window taller or shorter. Similar bars on the left, right, and bottom edges of the window may be used to move those edges in or out. Small L-shaped widgets in each corner will move the two adjoining edges simultaneously.

Adjacent to the title bar in the window shown in figure 18-2 are three additional widgets, one to the left and two to the right. Of the two on the right, the leftmost is the *iconify* widget. If you place the mouse pointer on this widget and depress the left mouse button, the window will change to an icon in the lower-left corner of the screen. While a window is displayed in *icon* form, the underlying process continues to run, but the user cannot interact with it. To restore an icon to its original form, place the arrow cursor on the icon and press the leftmost mouse button twice.

The other widget to the right of the title bar is the *maximize* widget. When you click on it with the leftmost mouse button, the selected window takes over the entire screen. The maximize widget thus has the opposite effect from that of the iconify widget. It makes the selected window as large as possible, while the iconify widget makes it as small as possible.

THE SYSTEM MENU

The widget to the left of the title bar accesses the System menu. When you place the cursor arrow on it and press the leftmost mouse button, the System menu pops up. The System menu provides an alternate method of performing many of the same tasks that you can perform with the other widgets.

The selections on the menu are: Restore, Move, Size, Minimize, Maximize, Lower, and Close. When the window is displayed at its normal size, the Restore option is in effect. To iconify the window, select Minimize. To fill the entire screen with the window, select Maximize. The Size option permits you to adjust the size of the window, without using the *maximize* and *iconify* widgets. The Move option allows movement of the entire window to another position on the screen, in the same way that clicking on the title bar does. The Close option causes the window to disappear and the process associated with it to stop running.

THE ROOT MENU = *Root*

Any implementation of X will have a menu that allows you to manipulate windows. In the SCO Xsight implementation, this menu is called the *Root*. It contains the following options: Clients, Xterm, Shuffle Up, Shuffle Down, Refresh, and Restart. The Clients option displays a submenu named the Clients menu. The Xterm option starts another terminal-emulator window. Shuffle Up brings to the fore a window that is partially or wholly obscured by another window. Shuffle Down places to the back a window that is obscuring other windows. Refresh redraws all the windows on the screen; you would use this option if your display had somehow become corrupted. The **Restart** option restarts the window manager and restores any icons to their original window form.

STARTING CLIENTS

Once you have one window running the **xterm** client, you can start additional clients from the terminal emulator by entering each of their names followed by an ampersand (**&**). This will start the client as a background process, causing a new window to pop up on the screen. For example, to start the calculator client **xcalc,** enter the command **xcalc&** at the command prompt in the **xterm** window. The calculator will appear on the screen, ready to perform a computation.

Another way of starting a client is to select it from a menu of client processes. In the SCO Xsight implementation, the Client menu (a submenu of the **Root** menu) displays the most frequently used clients. Selecting one with a mouse click starts it running and opens a window.

Figure 18-3 shows the Client menu along with its parent Root menu on a screen with a large number of windows already open.

STOPPING CLIENTS

You can stop a client by closing its window. Select the Close option from the System menu. The associated window will disappear from the screen, signifying that the client has stopped running. Another way is to use the **kill** command with the process ID of the client to be killed. A client's process ID is echoed to the screen when you start it as a background process from an **xterm** window.

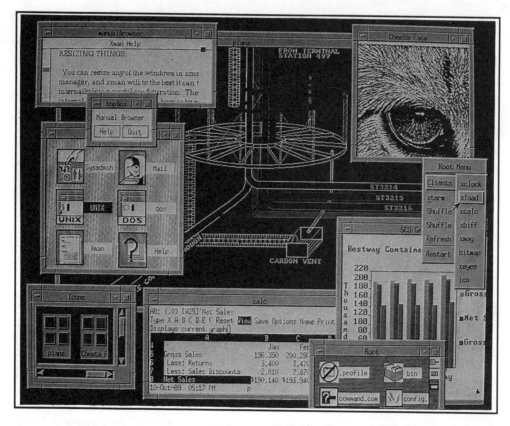

Figure 18-3. The Client menu after being pulled down from the Root menu

EXITING THE WINDOWING SYSTEM

The method of exiting the windowing system altogether and returning to the command line interface varies from one implementation of X to another. With SCO Xsight, pressing [Alt-SysReq] brings up a small dialog box, which asks, "Do you want to exit (y/n)?" If you press "y," any clients you may have started under X will be stopped and you will be returned to the $ prompt.

CUSTOMIZATION

The discussion so far in this chapter assumes that settings are left in their default conditions; however, you can customize some features of the window system, if you like, to match your preferences. For example, you can change the identity of the clients that are automatically started when X is started. If there are certain clients that you use on a regular basis, you can have them started automatically by making appropriate changes to the startup file. The name and location of this file depends on your implementation of X; consult your documentation to find it and determine how to modify it. Other things you can control are the appearance and behavior of your windows and the mapping of your keyboard and mouse. By setting the defaults for the clients that you customarily use, you can make sure these clients always appear in the form you like best.

Change the X environment to make it as comfortable as possible for its primary users. You may not want to make radical changes, though, in order to maintain compatibility with other X systems.

SUMMARY

Graphics-oriented windowing interfaces make computers much easier to operate. For an operating system as large and complex as Unix, a comprehensible user interface is especially important. Windowing environments do not come without a price, however; they consume considerable amounts of system resources.

The X Window system was developed as a universal windowing system to run on a wide variety of hardware platforms and operating systems. X has achieved widespread acceptance on Unix systems. Most major manufacturers of such systems have made X their windowing system of choice.

The X Window system is composed of two parts, the server and the clients, that work together to produce a graphical interface. The server interfaces directly with the computer hardware and controls the running of the clients. The clients are the applications, written to conform to the standard server interface, they do not need to be aware of what hardware they are running on. A properly written X client should run on any X system, regardless of the hardware platform.

Perhaps the most important client on any X system is the window manager, which determines the "look and feel" of the user interface. Additional clients such as system clock and pocket calculator are normally included with X. You can write new client applications with the help of the development toolkit, which contains a library of utilities useful in building applications.

Index

V

variables
  environment   133
  global   133
  local   133
  standard   135
vhand   15
vi   81
virtual handler process   15
virtual memory   15
VP/ix   179

W

wait   107
wall   99, 116
wc   120
while   141
who   95
who am i   96
widget   219, 221
wildcard   66
window manager   217, 219
windows   215
write   99, 116

X

X Window System   9, 216
xbiff   220
xcalc   220
xclock   219
Xenix   8
xinit   220
xload   219
xterm   219

Y

yank   86

teach yourself... the series

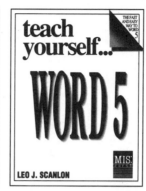

DOS cmd	Unix	DOS	Unix
ATTRIB	chmod	MKDIR	mkdir
Backup	cpio, tar	mode	stty, tty
Call	exec	more	more, pge
cd	cd	move	mv
CHDIR	cd	MSBACKUP	cpio tar
cls	clear	PATH	setenv, PATH(Cshe setpath (BorneShe
command	csh, sh	pause	sleep
comp	cmp, edit, diff	print	pr
CTTY	stty	prompt	PS 1
Dase	Dase	REM	#
Del	rm	Rename	move
Deltree	rm -r	Restore	cpio, tar
DIR	LS	RMDIR	rmdir
Doskey	history	set	env
echo	echo	SORT	sort
edit	vi	time	date
expand	uncompress unpack	TYPE	more, page, pg
FastHelp	apropos, man. what is	ver	uname
FC	edit, cmp, diff	XCOPY	cp
	— || —	XTREE	mkdir
FDisk			
Find	find		
FOR	for		
GOTO	GOTO (C shell)		
Help	apropos, man what is		
if	if (shell		